EGYPTIAN RESEARCH ACCOUNT.

FIFTH MEMOIR.

HIERAKONPOLIS

PART II.

BY

J. E. QUIBELL

AND

F. W. GREEN

LONDON:

BERNARD QUARITCH, 15, PICCADILLY, W.

1902.

CONTENTS.

CHAPTERS I.–V.

By F. W. Green.

INTRODUCTION.

SECT.		PAGE
1.	Difficulties of the work .	1
2.	Course of work . . .	1

CHAPTER I.

STRATIFICATION OF THE SITE.

3.	Lowest stratum . . .	1
4.	Second stratum . . .	2
5.	Third stratum	2
6.	Fourth stratum . . .	3
7.	Top stratum	3

CHAPTER II.

EARLIEST STONE WORK.

The circular revetment.

8.	Its construction . . .	3
9.	Its purpose	3
10.	The sections	4
11.	Results.	5

The inclined revetment.

12.	Its construction . . .	5
13.	Its age	5
14.	Its purpose	6

Stone walls and pavements.

15.	Walls by circular revetment	6
16.	Their purpose	6
17.	Rough stone pavements .	7
18.	The rows of stones . .	7

SECT.		PAGE
19.	System of the structures .	7
20.	Limestone pillars . . .	8

CHAPTER III.

THE TEMENOS AREA.

21.	West angle	8
22.	South-west side . . .	9
23.	The well	9
24.	Southern angle . . .	9
25.	South-east walls . . .	9
26.	Circular brick structures .	10
27.	Store rooms	10
28.	Granaries	11
29.	Later temple remains .	11
30.	North-east side . . .	11
31.	Minute Flints	11
32.	Wall levels and section .	12
33.	North angle	12
34.	Foundation deposit . .	13

CHAPTER IV.

DATE OF THE DEPOSIT AND TEMPLE.

35.	The main deposit . . .	13
36.	The brick temple . . .	14

CHAPTER V.

THE TOWN.

37.	The wall	15
38.	The gateways	15
39.	Archaic limestone statue .	15
40.	Age of the town wall . .	16
41.	The houses of the Old Kingdom	16
42.	The sealings	16
43.	Spindle whorls. . . .	17

SECT.		PAGE
44.	Vase-grinder's, House 89.	17
45.	Houses 145, 172	18
46.	Houses 205, 180, 211 . .	18
47.	House 144	18
48.	House 168, etc.	19

CHAPTER VI.

THE FORT.

By SOMERS CLARKE, F.S.A.

49.	Position and form . . .	19
50.	Material	20

CHAPTER VII.

THE CEMETERY.

By F. W. Green.

51.	Already worked . . .	20
52.	The painted tomb. . .	20
53.	The paintings	21
54.	The colours and condition	21
55.	Other graves	22
56.	Sizes of bricks	23

DESCRIPTION OF THE DISCOVERIES.

By J. E. Quibell.

CHAPTERS VIII.–XII.

CHAPTER VIII.

INTRODUCTORY.

57.	The conditions of the work	24
58.	Discussion by other writers	24
59.	The workers engaged . .	24

CONTENTS.

CHAPTER IX.

KOM EL AHMAR.

SECT.		PAGE
60.	Description of the site .	24
61.	The Fort	25
62.	The Kom	25
63.	The mastabas	25
64.	The cemetery	25
65.	The scattered pottery .	26

CHAPTER X.

THE TEMPLE.

66.	Site of town	26
67.	The gold hawk . . .	27
68.	The copper statues . .	27
69.	The pottery lion . . .	28
70.	The figure of Kha-sekhem	28

CHAPTER XI.

THE MAIN DEPOSIT.

SECT.		PAGE
71.	The group of archaic objects	28
72.	The heap of ivory, etc. .	29
73.	The maces, etc. . . .	30
74.	Catalogue of objects . .	30

CHAPTER XII.

THE AGE OF THE REMAINS.

75.	Date of the revetment .	33
76.	The brick walls . . .	33
77.	The gold hawk, and copper statues	33
78.	The main deposit . . .	33

SECT.		PAGE
79.	Uniform age of deposit .	34
80.	The order of burial . .	34

CHAPTER XIII.

DESCRIPTION OF THE PLATES   35
  Of the 1st season by J. E.
  Quibell.
  Of the 2nd season by
  F. W. Green.

CHAPTER XIV.

THE SEALINGS 54
  By F. Ll. Griffith, F.S.A.

INDEX 56
  By F. W. Green.

LIST OF PLATES.

These are in completion and continuation of the numbers published in "Hierakonpolis I."

		PAGE
I.	Limestone statue (kneeling) . . .	35
XXIII.	Head of sceptre and beads . .	39
XXVII.	Types of mace-heads . . .	41
XXVIII.	Lesser palette . . .	41
XXX.	Stone vases	43
XXXII.	Ape, grinder, etc. . .	43
XLVII.	Copper statue and hawk .	45
XLVIII A.	List of main deposit . .	28
XLVIII B.	„ „	
L.	Copper statue of Pepy . .	46
LI.	Copper bust, side view.	
LII.	„ „ ¾ view.	
LIII.	Copper statue of Pepy's son.	
LIV.	„ „ „	
LV.	„ head, side.	
LVI.	„ „ front.	
LVII.	Archaic limestone statue .	16, 47
LVIII.	Stele of Kha-sekhem . .	47
LIX.	Pieces of stone jars, etc. .	48
LX.	Flint knives, etc. . .	48

		PAGE
LXI.	Flint knives, etc. . .	48
LXII.	Vase grinders, etc. . .	49
LXIII.	Whorls, cylinders, and figures	49
LXIV.	Prehistoric objects . .	50
LXV.	Revetment, pillars, and drain.	50
LXVI.	Pottery. sceptre-head, and deposit .	50
LXVII.	Prehistoric tomb, etc. .	51
LXVIII.	Grinder's room, tomb, etc. .	51
LXIX.	Prehistoric and early pottery .	51
LXX.	Clay sealings . . .	17, 55
LXXI.	„ „	55
LXXII.	Large plan of temple .	9, 51
LXXIII.	Town enclosure, plan .	17
LXXIII A.	General plan . . .	54
LXXIV.	Fort plan	19
LXXV.	Painted tomb wall . .	20
LXXVI.	„ „ sect. A .	21
LXXVII.	„ „ sect. B .	21
LXXVIII.	„ „ sect. C .	21
LXXIX.	Figures from wall . .	21

INTRODUCTION.

1. THE importance of the results of Mr. Quibell's excavation at Hierakonpolis showed the necessity of further examination of the site, in order that any fragments of the inscribed mace-heads, or other objects of the archaic period that might have been scattered, should be recovered, as well as to make out, if possible, more fully the plan of the temple and other buildings.

The realisation of these objects was only partly fulfilled. Hardly any fragments of objects found in the previous season's work were recovered, nor was the plan of the temple made out as completely as was hoped.

The want of success in this direction was due in a great measure to the nature of the site; for, situated as it is within the area of inundation, it has been submitted to the action of water during several months in the year from a very distant period.

At the beginning of the work in December the water was still level with the foot of the enclosure walls, and even at the end of June it was met with less than two metres below them. Most of the pits and trenches dug in the preceding season had, in consequence of the water in them, collapsed, bringing down the walls which they exposed; this proved a great obstacle in recovering the plan.

2. As I had been fortunate enough to be with Mr. Quibell during the first season's work, it was decided (as he was unable to continue the exploration, owing to his appointment on the cataloguing staff of the Gizeh Museum) that the work should be put in my charge during the second season. This undertaking of the Egyptian Research Account was supplemented with a grant of £50 towards the expenses of the excavations, by the University of Cambridge, from the Wortz Fund.

The season's work proved of great interest, though the programme was not fully carried out, as no fragments of the inscribed maces were recovered; but part of a stele showing clearly the name scratched on the base of the small statuettes, a very archaic statue, as well as numerous archaic clay sealings, were found in the temple or town areas, and in the Prehistoric Cemetery a tomb decorated in colours was discovered.

CHAPTER I.

STRATIFICATION OF THE SITE.

3. BEFORE entering on a detailed account of the various parts of the temple and town areas, it will be better to give a short account of the strata met with in excavating the site; for in many cases the only clue to the date of the various structures examined depends wholly on the stratum in or on which they are built.

First, beginning from the lowest, is the old desert surface, at the depth of 5·0 metres below datum level; below this, indeed, traces of prehistoric pottery and charcoal were found, but all accurate observation was prevented owing to the water standing near this level, even at the end of the season: also, I am not sure that such remains are truly *in situ*, and that their depth is not to be attributed in great measure to the action of rain-water on the desert surface, washing down and burying such small objects as fragments of pottery and charcoal.

1ST STRATUM; DESERT SURFACE.

This desert surface consists of coarse sand with pebbles, above which were numerous flint flakes and fragments of prehistoric pottery. This condition of things may be seen anywhere on the present desert surface in the neighbourhood of the cemetery. As a definite surface, it was only well observed in the longitudinal sectional trench within the circular revetment, and between the two enclosure walls on the S.W. side of the temple.

To this level, in all probability, belong the prehistoric graves which were found on the site. One was discovered by Mr. Quibell partly under a wall running from the northernmost of the two rectangular masses of crude brick, or Pylons, towards the circular revetment. Another was found, during the second season's work, just outside the enclosure walls, 4·4 metres below datum level, on the N.E. side, opposite to the buildings under which the Principal Deposit was buried. This was the grave of a child about seven years old. The body was contracted, lying on its left side with the head to the N., in a circular pottery jar, or cist. Near the back, within the cist, was a small, rough, earthenware pot, mouth down. Close to, but outside, the cist was a long, slightly curved flint with a rounded butt and sharp point. As may be seen in the section, PL. LXXII., this is rather lower than the foundations of the Circular Revetment and the rough stone pavement near the revetted inclined plane.

What may be a third prehistoric burial was found under one of the walls of a group of houses, marked 89 on the plan of the Town Enclosure, and on the plan of the same group on PL. 68, room 5.

2ND STRATUM; ACCUMULATIONS.

4. Secondly, a rather ill-defined stratum, which represents the accumulation on the desert surface before the erection of any buildings that can now be identified. On this stratum rest the circular structure and the low-lying pavements. The depth of this stratum varies, the actual foot of the Circular Revetment being 4·2 metres below datum level.

It should be noticed that the revetted inclined plane which abuts on the S.W. wall begins about this level, and descends to a considerable depth below it.

Above this level the soil, though dark, is comparatively free from potsherds and charcoal, till the third stratum is reached.

3RD STRATUM; CHARCOAL-DISCOLOURED.

5. This stratum varies from 0·7 up to 1·0 metre above the old desert surface, or about 4·0 metres

below datum level; it is clearly defined and of very great extent, seeming to underlie the whole site of the town as well as the temple area. Towards the S.W. side of the temple enclosure, where the limestone pillars are situated, it thins out and is entirely absent within the Circular Revetment. As far as observed it attains its greatest thickness near the temple entrance on the N.E. side.

It is generally seen as a well-defined stratum of a deep black colour, owing to the amount of charcoal contained, 10 c.m. (4 inches) or more thick, but in places it is represented by lenticular patches of black, or fire-reddened earth. Throughout this account it is called "the charcoal-discoloured stratum." The materials composing it are chiefly charcoal, with numerous sherds of rough red prehistoric and IInd to IIIrd Dynasty pottery. This stratum was particularly rich in domestic objects of the early periods, and from it came the majority of the flint implements, limestone spindle whorls, some of which bore signs, and fragments of inscribed clay sealings; these last were of most frequent occurrence where the stratum attains its greatest observed thickness, near the N.E. entrance of the temple.

In the character of its contents the stratum is very similar to, though probably rather earlier than, the houses which were excavated in the town area, as they seem in most cases to have been built upon it.

The circular limestone block at the end of the passage projecting from the south side of the circular revetment, rests on crude brick walls, which form part of this stratum; these are evidently the remains of dwelling-houses, and it is to the inhabitants of such houses that the formation of this stratum is in all likelihood due. Similar remains of houses were found on this stratum under the outer N.E. enclosure wall, and at about the same level outside the temple enclosure wall near to where the prehistoric grave is situated.

The inscribed palettes, maces, votive bowls, ivory and other objects forming the main deposit, as well as the squatting limestone figures, and perhaps also the door socket, found by Mr. Quibell, seem in all probability to belong to the period of the formation of this charcoal-discoloured stratum; and I was of opinion, at the end of the second season's work, that they had been buried long anterior to the foundation of the crude brick temple. They seem to have been unsuspected by the later builders, except when a stray piece, such as the slate statue, or stela of Kha-sekhem, happened to be found during the digging of the new foundations, when they were either buried in the new sanctuary or thrown aside.

4TH STRATUM; DARK EARTH.

6. Above the charcoal-discoloured stratum the earth is comparatively free from charcoal and pottery, though it is of a dark colour, till a stratum, also discoloured by charcoal, but not so strongly marked as the last, is met with at 0·6 m. (2 feet) above the charcoal-discoloured stratum, or on the average 2·75 metres below datum level.

It is most conspicuous in the southern quarter of the temple enclosure where near, and under the walls it exhibits a tendency to divide and enclose lenticular patches of comparatively clean loam, as if this part of the site had been used in early times as a rubbish heap.

There is very little difference in character between this and the charcoal-discoloured stratum below it; judging by the objects contained in them, both belong to the early dynastic period, the upper one being probably contemporary with the majority of the dwelling-houses which occupy the town area, in which sealings of Kha-ba, Neter-khet, and Seneferu were found.

7. Above the fourth stratum the earth is comparatively free from charcoal, etc., for a height of 0·6 metre (2 feet). But as the ground has here been prepared for the crude brick buildings by cutting down the revetments, breaking off the pillars, and is generally disturbed to the same end, little importance can be attached to it as a stratum. In places thin layers of white sand occur, marking the foundation level of the new temple. The general depth of the foot of the crude brick walls is 2·3 metres below datum level, but in some cases it is greater, as may be seen in the section. The thick crude brick wall, which has been skewed to avoid covering the parallel rows of stones on the S.W. side of the temple, has its foot only 0·2 m. above them. And some of the walls of the group of rooms under which the main deposit was found descend to a depth of 3 metres below datum level.

But these are exceptions; the general depth of the crude brick walls is 2·3 metres below datum level, and this fact, together with the size of the bricks (which is practically the same throughout the building), is strong evidence of their having been built from one design.

Above the level of the bases of the walls the earth has been disturbed so much by *sebakhin* and others as to render it useless for the purpose of dating, except in so far as it gives an idea of the amount of disturbance that has taken place since the destruction of the temple.

CHAPTER II.

THE EARLIEST STONEWORK.

THE CIRCULAR REVETMENT.

8. IN the centre of the temple enclosure is a mound cased with rough stones, the circular plan of which may have suggested the hieroglyphic sign for the town of Nekhen.

The casing or Revetment which is but one block thick, is built of natural fragments of Nubian sandstone, such as may be seen lying on the desert surface in the neighbourhood; they are set together without mortar of any kind, the dark earth which is now seen between the stones having probably drifted in from the outside.

The blocks are nearly equal in size, their average dimensions being 30 × 20 × 8 c.m. (or a foot × 8 ins. × 3 ins.), selected with a certain amount of care and laid in horizontal courses, but no attempt has been made to make them truly horizontal. Each course is set back about 8 c.m. (3 ins.) from the face of the course below, thus making a step 8 c.m. (3 ins.) wide and as much high, the general slope of the whole being 45°.

The appearance of this revetment is that of a flight of steps, but this is certainly not the purpose of the stonework, as the tread of each step is too narrow, and the angle of slope too steep; nor is the construction of sufficient strength to stand the strain to which it would be subjected if used as stairs.

9. The purpose of the stonework was evident as soon as the ground enclosed within it came to be examined: it was then seen that the stones formed the Revetment of a mound of desert sand.

Originally the Revetment must have been higher than at present; but it has been cut down at the time when the ground was levelled previously to building the crude brick temple. The upper course on the south side is now 0·5 m. above the foot of the sanctuary walls, and level with the upper surface of the crude brick floor of the passage on the south side of the row of sanctuary chambers, the same pavement which probably extended over the whole area of the temple.

The lowest course of this revetment rests upon the archaic strata 2·0 m. below the foot of the later crude brick constructions, and 0·6 above the original desert surface; it is therefore below the level of the charcoal-discoloured stratum, containing the seals, flint knives and archaic pottery.

The complete plan of this curious structure could not be recovered entirely, as the space within the enclosure on the North side of the sanctuary has been denuded to a depth lower than that of the foot of the crude brick walls, thus exposing the Revetment to the depredations of natives seeking for building materials. Nothing was found, though trenches as deep as the water level were run across the ground where the Revetment should have been met with; and on following the course of the revetment itself, all traces were lost as soon as the low ground was approached.

10. To ascertain the nature of this revetted mound, a sectional trench, about two metres wide, was run almost coincident with the temple axis from a point two metres north of the north wall of the sanctuary, to a point immediately behind the south face of the revetment.

The following was the section exhibited on the North side of the sanctuary :—

		c.m.
Recent accumulations.	Earth black and dirty; with large fragments of baked clay, or brick, little or no pottery . . .	10
	Soil lighter in colour; numerous sandstone chips, charcoal, potsherds, and a fragment of bone . .	30
	Layer of blackened earth with charcoal; fragments of burnt brick, and chips of sand stone . . .	60
	Crude Brick pavement resting on ground level, with footings of wall	80

Below pavement, clean whitish sand.

Inside the sanctuary chamber, where the golden-headed hawk was found, and just below the footings of the walls, were a few crude bricks 28 × 11 × 8 c.m. (11 × 4·3 × 3·1 ins.), resting in clean sand, free from charcoal and potsherds. These bricks had evidently fallen in, they were not *in situ*.

On the south side of this chamber, beginning from immediately below the crude brick pavement, the following section was observed :—

—	Below Footings of Sanctuary Walls.	Below Datum Level.
	Met.	Met.
Very sandy loam, with small lumps of yellow clay; a few fragments of either prehistoric or Old Kingdom coarse red pottery, a few fragments of prehistoric polished red ware; traces of charcoal . . .	1·6	3·9
Fragment of prehistoric rough red ware at . . .	2·2	4·5
Fragment of prehistoric shell bangle (found by workmen) at	2·4	4·7
Old desert surface. Band of coarse sand, with occasional pebbles 3 c.m. in diameter, and lenticules of sandy clay . . .	2·7	5·0
Dark coloured flint flake; fragment of prehistoric rough red pottery; fragment of prehistoric black-topped ware at	2·8	5·1
At this level (5·1) prehistoric pottery, both rough-faced red, and black-topped ware, as well as flint flakes. This character continues down until water level at being reached, March 31st, 1899, prevented further examination.	3·4	5·7

The following section was observed about 2.0 metres north of the revetment :—

—	Below Footing of Sanctuary.	Below Datum Level.
	Met.	Met.
Débris of modern hut, dark earth with chips of lime stone and potsherds of late periods, etc. Down to .	0·3	2·6
White sand with numerous specks of charcoal.		
Fragments of small brick approximately x × 11 × 8. Fragments of prehistoric black-topped pottery, on one of which was a design rudely scratched on the baked clay. Fragments of prehistoric ash jars and flint flakes	1·1	3·4
White sand, with occasional patches of yellow sand. A few fragments of prehistoric rough red pottery.		
Old desert surface . . . . . . Coarse sand with pebbles; fragments of prehistoric black-topped pottery; fragments of large jar of rough red pottery; lumps of baked clay. The old desert surface has a slight dip to South.	2·6	4·9
Water level, March 31st, 1899	3·4	5·7

Immediately behind the inner face of the Revetment on the south side the following section was observed :—

—	Below Datum Level.
	Metres.
Stones of Revetment bedded in sand, with a little dark earth behind this clean white sand	2·0
Fragments of rough prehistoric pottery, and a few specks of charcoal	3·0
Clean white sand Footing of Revetment	4·2
Fragment of rough red prehistoric pottery at . . .	4·9
Fragment of rough red prehistoric pottery and small piece of charcoal at	5·2
Soil more sandy, with lumps of yellow clay, numerous fragments of rough red prehistoric pottery, and a few fragments of polished red prehistoric pottery	5·6
Stratum of gravel and sand.	
Fragment of prehistoric circular earthenware cist.	
Water level, March 5th, 1899	5·7

11. The points to be noticed are as follow:

(1). The original desert surface occurs at a depth of from 5·1 to 5·3 metres below datum level or from 2·8 to 3·0 metres below the footing of the main brick structure, the highest part of which is at a point near the south side of the Revetment. This shows that the mound is purely artificial, and does not rest on any natural feature as a base.

(2). The remarkable cleanness of the sand composing the mound, hardly any remains occurring till the original desert surface is reached.

(3). The fragments of brick met with are those of small bricks, such as are found used in the IInd or IIIrd Dynasty dwelling-houses excavated within the town enclosure, as well as bricks from the walls of prehistoric graves in the neighbouring cemetery.

Modern Arab bricks are also of about the same size, but we may dismiss the supposition that these are of such a late date, as they were found at too great a depth.

(4). The only pottery that was found belonged to the prehistoric period.

(5). The total absence of the charcoal-discoloured stratum.

The frequent occurrence of prehistoric pottery and flint flakes on the old desert surface, points to a considerable time having elapsed before the construction of the Circular Revetment; and also perhaps to its not having been a sacred site at that early period. The absence of the charcoal-discoloured stratum in which are flint implements and clay seals of the IInd or IIIrd Dynasty, gives us a date anterior to which its

construction must be assigned. Thus, somewhere at the beginning of the Ist Dynasty seems then to be the date of the building of the Revetted mound.

The drawing by Mr. Somers Clarke on Plate LXV. give a very good idea of the south face of the revetment. The rough sandstone blocks of which it is built are, however, made to appear more regular in shape than they actually are.

THE INCLINED REVETMENT.

12. In the eastern quarter of the temple enclosure, are remains of another revetment. It consists of horizontal courses of rough Nubian sandstone blocks, similar to those of the Circular Revetment. The highest course is 3·3 metres below datum level, and 0·8 metre below the footing of the inner enclosure wall and pavement abutting on it. Each succeeding course is set back, forming a step 23 c.m. (9 ins.) wide by 8 c.m. (3 ins.) high, the general angle of slope being 19°, but as the lower courses are reached the slope is somewhat steeper.

The depth of the lowest course was not ascertained, as it exceeded 4·8 metres below datum level at which point water was reached 4·2·99. The presence of the water caused the collapse of the sides of the pit, so that without re-excavating the spot anew it was not possible to reach the foot of this revetment.

13. The structure appears to curve inwards, that is to say, as if it formed part of the lining of a large cone-shaped depression; but this shape may be caused by the thrust of the earth behind, when the face was unburied. The border towards the middle of the enclosure is rough and unfinished, or the stones have been removed; that nearest the enclosure wall is well defined, stopping abruptly in the vertical plane of the inner face of the enclosure wall.

This suggests that it is later than the wall, but the following point seems to be against this supposition. Below the foot of the walls and pavement is a layer of pottery and charcoal, about 10 or 20 c.m. thick, on which the wall was founded, resting on a stratum of dark earth 60 c.m. thick containing little or no pottery. Below this the dark charcoal-discoloured stratum is reached, which passes uninterruptedly over the revetment, and under the wall: but the top of the revetment may have projected through it. If the revetment had been later than the wall the charcoal-discoloured stratum must have been removed in order to build it.

Lying on the fourth course from the top was a broken, rough, Old Kingdom earthenware jar with a pointed base. Excepting a few flint flakes, such as are found everywhere in the low levels, this jar was all that was observed in contact with this revetment.

It is possible that the revetment was known in some way to the builders of the later temple, who enclosed it within their temenos, avoiding covering it up, in the same way as has been done in the case of the parallel rows of stones on the N.W. side of the temple area.

14. The purpose of this revetment is not clear. It may have been an inclined plane descending to a well, or pool which was filled up at an early date, or when the well now in use was dug ; or perhaps there were originally two wells situated symmetrically on each side of the axis, one of which continued to be used down to later times. Against either of these suppositions is the fact that the structure seems too weak for the strain it would have to bear if much walked upon.

STONE WALLS AND PAVEMENTS.

15. Ten metres to the west of the main axis of the temple, two walls similar in materials and workmanship to the circular Revetment, project from its southern face. These walls are not parallel, but tend to converge to a point to the south. At ten metres measured from the top course of the revetment, they are joined by a cross-wall, thus forming a blind passage. The inner sides of these walls are the true faces, the outer being extremely uneven. Their highest remaining courses are level, or nearly so, with the topmost course of the circular Revetment. These walls, which descend but a few centimetres below this level, where they touch the revetment, increase in depth as they extend southward, till at the junction with the cross-wall they rest on ground 1·0 metre below this level. The foot of each wall rests entirely in the earth, and does not touch the revetment anywhere except at the northern end.

The foot of the cross-wall is rather lower than the side walls and stands on a hard surface of rammed earth or pavement, on which are traces of crude brick

walls of an early date, resting on the charcoal-discoloured stratum.

At the closed end of this passage and partly under the walls, is a circular block of limestone, very similar to a millstone in shape, having a slight depression on its upper surface.

16. The purpose of these walls, seems to be to revet the sides of a passage leading down to the circular limestone block, but with what object, it is difficult to determine. If this be the object of these walls, they must have been built at a period when the accumulation of earth on the site had raised its surface at least as high as the still remaining courses, or their purpose as a revetment or retaining wall would not have been fulfilled.

They have undergone the same cutting-down process to make room for the foundations of the crude brick temple, as the circular revetment, which proves them to be anterior to the brickwork.

To what height the surface of the soil had risen by the time of the New Kingdom, which seems to be the probable date of the crude brick temple walls, I am unable to say.

It may be observed that the axis of this structure is not square with the face of the revetment at the point where the axis cuts it. Its axis, if produced towards the North, passes through the chamber in which the golden headed hawk was found, and if produced to the Southward passes near to the well, and to the remains of a rough pavement lying in the archaic level near the enclosure wall. Also if the angle which this line makes with the main axis of the temple, be laid off on the East side of the main axis, it will pass through the rough stairway-like stonework at the East angle of the temple. Of course this may be merely coincidence, but as it is difficult to make out the relations between the different archaic structures, it may be worth recording.

At a point roughly at right angles to the main axis of the temple, in contact with the East side of the circular revetment, are remains of two parallel walls of rough stone ; these may be all that is left of another similar blind passage. These walls are, however, in too dilapidated a condition to show their purpose. The width of the passage they would form, is rather narrower than that of the structure just mentioned.

No other stonework was observed in contact with the circular Revetment.

ROUGH STONE PAVEMENTS, ETC.

17. In the eastern quarter of the temple enclosure, ten metres from the inner enclosure-wall, are remains of a rough pavement.

The depth is 4·15 metres below datum level, and therefore at the same depth as the foot of the circular Revetment. This seems to show that this was the ground level at one time, and that the foot of the circular revetment does not rest in a trench dug for its foundations, but that the lowest courses were merely laid on what was then the surface of the soil.

Very little now remains of this pavement, the stones are (like those of all these low-lying constructions), rough natural Nubian sandstone blocks, undressed, and laid without much care.

18. On the western side of the temple enclosure, close against the plane of the face, but 0·2 c.m. below the foot of a thick crude brick wall, are two parallel rows of rough undressed Nubian sandstone blocks, resting on the archaic stratum 3·5 metres below datum level, or 1·0 below the foot of the sanctuary walls. Their general direction makes a small angle with the temple axis and later buildings. The face of the thick crude brick wall has been slightly skewed, so as to follow their direction, perhaps to avoid covering them, while at the same time keeping as close as possible to their outer face. The rest of the wall is parallel to the temple axis. The row stops just below a thinner cross-wall, which is at a lower level than other crude brick walls, and may possibly be earlier. The dimensions of the bricks composing it are 37 ? × 19 ? × 11 c.m. There was no evidence to show that the parallel row of stones formed the foot of a crude brick or other kind of wall.

Six metres beyond these rows is another patch of rough stone work, resting on the charcoal-discoloured stratum. The direction is at right angles or nearly so to the parallel row of stones just mentioned. The end of this short row, which is in line with the long parallel row, is laid on ground of the same level, but as it nears the circular revetment it tends to ascend. The small detached patch of stonework still further to the N.W. is level with the higher end of this group.

The cross row seems to be part of an inclined pavement leading from the level of the long parallel row to a pavement at a rather higher level.

These parallel rows of rough blocks probably run further to the N.W. than is shown in the plan ; but as the site is occupied by native houses at this point it was deemed inexpedient to incur the expense necessary to continue the trenches in this direction.

At a point near the well close against the inner enclosure wall, are the remains of another pavement of rough stone blocks. The level of this is higher than the rest of the work of a similar character, being only 2·7 metres below datum level, and is therefore more nearly on a level with the circular limestone block at the end of the revetted passage than is the rest of the rough stonework. Not enough remains, however, for any exact estimate of its relation with the other early structures to be made out.

Near the spot where Mr. Quibell found the great inscribed palette, and probably in some relation with it, is a rectangular slab of limestone with a shallow rectangular depression on its upper surface. Close to this slab is a row of stones which may have formed part of some structure since destroyed. The level of this group, which rest on the charcoal-discoloured stratum, is that of the circular limestone block at the end of the revetted passage, so they should be attributed to the period when that addition was made to the central structure ; and it seemed to me as before stated that all the objects belonging to the main deposit, as well as the squatting statues and door socket, should be ascribed to this period, and not to the earlier period when the revetted mound was heaped together.

19. The archaic structures which have been just described may when complete have formed at the earliest period a building something as follows. A circular, or nearly circular, revetted mound or platform, on which may have stood a shrine like that depicted on one of the Old Kingdom Mastabas in the Gizeh Museum. Extending from the base of the mound on all sides, but especially to the S.E., stretched a pavement ; this may have been only of hard earth, with the parts most subject to wear, such as the approach to the wells, made of rough stones. Though it should be noticed that, judging by the levels, only the small patch of pavement 10 metres from the revetted inclined plane seems contemporary with the circular Revetment ; the rest of the pavements seem rather to belong to the period when the revetted passage was added to the central structure.

The pillars, too, seem to belong to this second period rather than to the first.

At certain places, rude pillars, or perhaps statues, were set up, the bases of which are described below.

By the second or third dynasty this primitive temple had been encroached upon and heaped round by habitations of this period, leaving the mound rising above the new accumulation.

It is to this second period that the objects found by Mr. Quibell would seem to belong.

LIMESTONE PILLARS.

20. Close, and evidently related in some way, to the row of stones, are two rough limestone pillars (see plan and PL. LXV.) standing in the same archaic stratum on which the long rows are laid. The one figured on the upper part of the plate is the larger. Its base rests in clean sand just below the level of the charcoal-discoloured stratum. Near the base are some rough angular blocks of Nubian sandstone, which form a sort of socket for the pillar. These blocks are on nearly the same level as the ground on which the parallel rows of stones are laid.

Among the interstices of these socket stones fragments of coarse red, and polished red, prehistoric pottery were found.

The upper part of the pillar has been broken off exhibiting a conchoidal fracture; the top is now 2·6 metres below datum level, and level with a stratum of clean white sand 10 or 20 c.m. thick which is probably the sand bed for the foundations of the later crude brick buildings.

On the S.E. side of the pillar 55 c.m. from the top, is a mark that may have been produced by abrasion such as may be seen on ancient buildings like the temple of Edfu, or may have been produced by a blow from an axe, or other sharp instrument, the cut produced having been altered by the action of the surrounding damp soil.

Another somewhat smaller limestone pillar was found further to the S.W. (see PL. LXV. the upper of the two drawings). The base was sunk less deeply than the other pillar. Three rough sandstone blocks formed a socket, at nearly the same level as the other. · Close by, in the stratum in which its base rests, a fragment of prehistoric pottery decorated with red wavy lines, was found. The top of this pillar also, had been broken off, the top is now 2·5 metres below

datum line which is practically the same depth as the other.

Two other pillars were found in the previous year by Mr. Quibell. One was situated close to the revetted passage that projects from the south face of the circular Revetment, and another below the bases of the sandstone columns that occupy the space near the temple well.

It may be that these pillars are the lower portions of rude statues, such as were found by Professor Petrie at Kuft, and at the northern gateway of the town during the present excavations.

On the plan and sections all early work is shown in black.

Though the section was made along the lines marked on the plan, nevertheless all archaic stone-work is shown even if it be behind the plane of the section, in which case the section may be regarded as an elevation. The brick walls which are later have not been so treated.

CHAPTER III.

THE TEMENOS AREA.

WEST ANGLE.

21. THE western angle of the temple enclosure is occupied by a number of native houses; these it was not deemed expedient to pull down for the sake of the rough stone-work, as nothing else (except pottery, and a few New Kingdom scarabs of very poor quality) was found in this quarter of the temple.

A small doll of dark-coloured baked clay was found here, level with, or slightly lower than, the foot of the temple walls. Such clay dolls belong to the period between the end of the Middle Kingdom and the beginning of the XVIIIth Dynasty: as evidence for the date of the crude brick temple this is important, and it has therefore been figured on PL. LXVI.

There never seems to have been much in the way of buildings in this quarter of the temple: it is also unprofitable, because the surface has been denuded to such an extent that water stands in places during the season of inundation.

In the lower strata only a few fragments of prehistoric pottery and charcoal were found: in which respect the strata here form a marked contrast to their representatives in other quarters of the temple area.

S.W. Side of Temenos.

22. On the South Western side of the temple enclosure little was found except the walls, the low-lying stone-work, and the rough limestone pillars. The upper layers resulted from habitations of Roman or Coptic times, as was shown by numerous fragments of domestic pottery of that period. Of the houses themselves, little remains except the floors, and the broken cooking pots, many of which are blackened by fire. In some places drains descend from the level of the floors to the depth of the foot of the crude brick walls of the temple. These drains are made by a series of tall pottery jars, fitted end to end, the bottom of each being broken off and fitted into the mouth of the one below. A drawing of the best example is shown on Pl. LXV.

In a quantity of rubbish, consisting chiefly of pottery of this period, which had been deposited in a hole in the floor of one of the huts, were numerous fragments of XVIIIth Dynasty pottery decorated in blue, a piece of prehistoric slate palette, and the handle of an alabaster jar, in the form of a snake's head, which seems from its technique to belong to the archaic period. This object is illustrated on Pl. LIX. 3.

The Well.

23. In that quarter of the temple area in which the well is situated, no structure belonging to the archaic period was found, except the rough stone pavement. There were, however, such small objects as flint flakes, and fragments of pottery, which are met with in both the charcoal-discoloured stratum (third stratum), and the one above it (fourth stratum).

The well itself cuts through these two strata, the section thus exposed showing them with great clearness.

The stairway leading down to the well was completely cleared during the second season's work; but nothing was found except a few earthenware vessels of Roman or Coptic date; the continual presence of water in the well prevented any extensive exploration in this direction.

The stone-work of the well and stairway is good, the sandstone blocks of the building being carefully squared and fitted together. The general slope of the steps is 1:2.

Outside that part of the outer enclosure wall which is nearest to the well, is a mass of broken water jars, resting on what must have been the ground level when the temple was rebuilt. The earth on which this mass rested contained pottery and flint flakes of the archaic period. The mass of pottery which has evidently been thrown out from the well consists of jars of the New Kingdom. At the bottom of the mass was a piece of green glaze of the same period. No piece which could be definitely assigned to the Middle Kingdom was observed, but Middle Kingdom and Early New Kingdom water jars, such as these seem to be, do not present sufficient differentiation to enable me to state positively that no Middle Kingdom pottery was present.

Southern Angle.

24. The Southern angle of the temple enclosure appears to have been broken away. There are also traces of walls, which may be of earlier date, perhaps part of the town wall.

Traces of a crude brick pavement were met with here; this does not seem to have formed part of that which occurs on the outside of the enclosure walls near the circular pits. Its surface had a strong dip towards the broken angle. This pavement may be of comparatively recent date.

Well outside the temple enclosure, towards the S.E., several walls are shown on the town plan. These seem to be generally earlier than the enclosure, and are related in some way to the town wall.

South East Walls.

25. The South East side of the temple is bounded by two parallel enclosure walls, the outer 1·0 metre (39 ins.), the inner 0·8 metre (31 ins.) thick. Their bases rest on a bed of broken pottery a few c.m. (a couple of inches) thick.

The space between these two walls has a flooring, of crude bricks 30 c.m. (a foot) thick; its upper surface is level with the remains of the temple pavement within the enclosure.

Above this floor another similar floor has been laid, with its upper surface 0·5 metre higher than that of the lower pavement or floor.

No evidence was observed that either of these crude brick floors had been paved with stone.

Beyond a few fragments of pottery, of apparently the New Kingdom, no object of interest was found

c

on these floors: but below them, chiefly in the charcoal-discoloured stratum, numerous flint implements and inscribed clay sealings were found.

CIRCULAR BRICK STRUCTURES.

26. Close against the middle point of the outer enclosure wall, on the south western side, are two circular crude brick structures, or brick-lined pits, which seem to have had their mouths level with a crude brick pavement, of which traces were found outside the enclosure walls, and which, when complete, may have surrounded the temple.

The walls of these pits descend to a considerable depth below the foot of the temple walls, resting almost on the higher charcoal-discoloured stratum (fourth stratum). The bricks of which they are built are very nearly the same size as those of the main building.

Both pits had two floors; the lowest level with the foot of their walls, and another rather lower than the upper of the two floors between the enclosure walls.

Under the lower floors occur objects of the archaic period, such as fragments of alabaster vases, limestone spindle whorls and inscribed clay sealings. Between the two floors pottery, flints, and other objects of the Old Kingdom, were found. On, and above the upper floors all the pottery belonged to well known New Kingdom types.

It is possible that these two structures do not belong to the temple as we now see it, but to some part of the Old Kingdom buildings; and that they were repaired, and higher level floors added at some time during the New Kingdom.

Similar, but smaller, structures are met with in other parts of the temple enclosure, some of which may be early: but one which is seen to cut through the circular revetment is at any rate later than that work; while another, of rather larger diameter, cuts through one of the crude brick walls of the temple itself, near to where the main deposit was found.

Resting on the pavement between the two circular pits, and associated with pottery of the New Kingdom, were a great number of long-shaped earthenware vessels filled with white ashes.

These vessels, which are of coarse red pottery, were from 18 to 20 c.m. (7 to 8 ins.) long, 5 c.m. (2 ins.) wide at the top, and the base rounded. Though more than a score were found, only one or two were complete, nearly all had been broken across

the middle and thrown together. The wood ash generally remains inside.

A very great number of fragments of the same kind of vase are to be seen near the temples within the Great Wall of El Kab, on the east bank, where they undoubtedly belong to the New Kingdom.

What purpose they served is not clear; they seem more in the nature of a case or sheath than a vase proper.

Near to the eastmost of these circular pits, and eight and a half metres from the outer enclosure wall, was found the large alabaster vase figured on PL. LIX. 2; it lay 2·6 metres below datum level, resting on what must have been the surface of the ground at some time during the Old Kingdom. Between these two walls, at a point about 5 metres S.W. of the axis, but below the level of their foot, was found part of a porphyry vase, with the *Ka* name Khasekhemui roughly scratched upon it. This inscription is figured on PL. LIX. 8.

STORE ROOMS.

27. Abutting on the inner of these two walls is a row of short cross-walls, which seem to have been parts of a series of store rooms, most of which have now been destroyed. On the floors, and in the angles of these rooms, were numerous earthenware jars, and ring-shaped pot stands of the New Kingdom. In one of the jars a rough glazed scarab of Thothmes III was found.

Lying transversely across two of these partition walls are two blocks of a granite similar to that bearing the inscription of King Khasekhemui, and to the door sill at the east entrance. That which is seen on the plan lying the closer to the wall, seems to be a rough stela of peculiar shape, its dimensions are about 2·6 × 0·85 × 0·9 metres (102 × 33 × 35 ins.). The lower 0·35 m. (14 ins.) has a foot-like projection. The surfaces, except the base, which is quite rough, have been only hammer-dressed, and are by no means true planes. The top is roughly semi-circular. None of the faces have been finished or inscribed. The other granite block, lying near it, has been so broken and defaced as to be little better than a formless mass, but it had been squared and faced up originally. Both blocks rest on earth slightly above the flooring of the rooms, which forms part of the crude brick pavement of the temple.

Part of a stela, bearing the *Ka* name of Khasekhem, was found 40 c.m. higher than the base of this granite stela, in the earth that has accumulated in the angle formed by the partition wall, against which it rests, and the inner enclosure wall : and 50 c.m. below it (that is practically on the floor of the same store room) was found part of the plinth of a small archaic statuette in limestone, similar in work to those of Kha-sekhem, found by Mr. Quibell. This fragment is figured on PL. LIX. 1.

One metre below the pavement at this point, and in the charcoal-discoloured stratum, three crescent-shaped flints and several scrapers were found.

GRANARIES.

28. The crude brick pavement of the temple is pierced in the east angle by four crude brick granaries, shown on the plan. Their mouths are flush with the pavement : and the sandstone slab, that formed the stopper, was found in position, in one case.

The bottom of these granaries was lined with hard beaten earth. All were empty except for a few flint flakes, and part of a baboon in green glaze of the archaic period which was found in one of them.

Close to these granaries, on the pavement, were many fragments of pottery, part of a pink and white breccia bowl, an earthenware net sinker, which may be of late date, a broken piece of glaze decoration resembling a thistle, and part of a green glaze ring bearing the name of Amenhotep III.

Within the enclosure, and ten metres from these granaries in a direction parallel to the temple axis, there descended from the pavement level a pit about 2 metres deep, filled chiefly with kitchen refuse. Among a number of fragments of New Kingdom pottery, at the bottom of this pit or rubbish shoot, was part of an uraeus in copper or bronze, with traces of gilding, part of a small alabaster vase with the cartouche of Necho (Uhem-ab-ra) of the XXVIth Dynasty, and a small piece of wrought iron.

Owing to the piece of iron being associated with such a miscellaneous collection of objects no definite period can, unfortunately, be assigned to it.

LATER TEMPLE REMAINS.

29. The area between the temenos walls on the south west side and the circular revetment, has been so denuded by sebakhin that the present ground surface, except where the débris of walls have added to its height, is only about 0·5 m. above the level

of the temple pavement. The stones which once formed it have almost all disappeared ; those that still remain *in situ* are shown on the plan. As far as could be seen the pavement consisted of sandstone slabs, some of which originally belonged to some former temple or addition to the primitive temple ; on the under side of one of them is the cartouche of Sebekhotep, and on what was also probably a similar slab Mr. Quibell found the cartouche of one of the Antefs.

Part of what was probably the sandstone facing of the crude brick walls is seen adhering to one of the two rectangular masses of crude brick, or pylons. Between these, Mr. Quibell found a sandstone architrave bearing the cartouche of Thothmes III.

NORTH EAST SIDE.

30. At the eastern angle of the temple are several walls, of varying thickness, parallel to the enclosure ; some of these may be of earlier date than the temple walls.

A sandstone paved way runs from the temple enclosure to the outer of these walls.

The space or passage between the inner (or thicker) enclosure wall, and the outer (thinner) one, has been paved with crude bricks, at two distinct levels. The lower pavement rests on the same ground as the foot of the walls ; the upper has been built on an accumulation of earth 1·0 m. thick. The distance separating them is the same as that between the two pavements found in the two circular pits. Also, as in those pits, there lay over the lower pavement numerous objects of the Old Kingdom, and even earlier periods, such as pottery, flint flakes, inscribed sealings, and a fragment of alabaster bowl bearing the same dedicatory inscription as the large granite and alabaster jars.

On the upper pavement nearly all the objects found belonged to the New Kingdom, one XVIIIth Dynasty scarab of blue glaze being among them.

MINUTE FLINTS.

31. Seven metres along the third wall (reckoned from the innermost) is a hollow, excavated partly in the wall, and partly in the earth which fills the space between the two pavements. This cavity is like the *Khasna* or primitive locker of a modern Egyptian house, and evidently served the same purpose.

The upper pavement passed uninterruptedly over

the mouth of this cavity, and its floor was laid with hard beaten earth. At the bottom of this cavity an enormous number of exceedingly small pointed flint implements were found; and with them were many broken carnelian pebbles, some chipped into the form of rough beads, one or two of which showed signs of the commencement of the boring operation; also chips of amethyst and rock-crystal, and one or two flakes of greenish black obsidian. Other collections of these small flint points, and materials from which beads are made, were found between this place and the granite block at the entrance to the temple; they occurred invariably level with the lower floor of the passage between the two walls. These flint points seem to be drills for boring carnelian, amethyst, and other beads, but how this was accomplished is not evident.

What is difficult to account for is that such objects, which seem to belong to the Old Kingdom, should be found in a cavity in what seems (judging by its parallelism with the main structure, and the size of the bricks) to be an XVIIIth Dynasty wall; but unfortunately the size of the bricks was not determined with sufficient accuracy to put the last statement beyond doubt.

Set in the lower of these two floors, near the granite block, were two pots of the Old Kingdom; this seems to show that the lower floor at any rate, should be assigned to the same period, unless we assume that these pots were in use at a later date.

Perhaps the original temple was surrounded by walls which were not completely removed, as all the work in the interior of the enclosure seems to have been, but were merely altered to suit the new requirements.

The charcoal-discoloured stratum occurs below the lower floor or pavement.

Near the granite door sill of the N.E. entrance are a series of depressions in the upper crude brick floor; these may be all that is left of holes into which the lower ends of flag-staffs were stepped.

WALL LEVELS AND SECTION.

32. From the section it will be seen that the first or inner enclosure wall, and the thick second wall, have their footing at a greater depth than that of most of the interior walls of the temple.

The thick wall whose foot is 2·8 metres below datum level, rests on a charcoal-discoloured stratum, already referred to as the fourth stratum, the thick-

ness of which is here from 30 c.m. to 40 c.m. In this stratum, on this side of the temple, many inscribed clay sealings were found, as well as flint flakes and pottery of the early period. Inscribed seals were also found at much higher levels, often higher than the foot of the wall; but these seals evidently come from the archaic stratum, and owe their present position to the general disturbance of the site that took place during the building of the crude brick walls.

The third, or charcoal-discoloured stratum, is met with at a depth of from 3·3 to 3·4 metres below datum level; and in this stratum also, as in that immediately above it, numerous flint knives, flakes, and inscribed clay sealings were found.

Below this stratum all objects met with belong to the prehistoric period proper, such as polished red and black-topped ware. The old desert surface was reached 3·0 metres below the foot of the enclosure wall.

The accompanying section shows the succession and depths of the various strata :—

—	Below Datum Level.
	Metres.
Foot of thick enclosure wall at	2·7
Stratum 30 c.m. thick, composed chiefly of fragments of coarse pottery and charcoal. The fragments being chiefly those of prehistoric earthenware trays, and of pots with pointed base, such as were found in the houses in the town area (see lower half of PL. LXIX.) belong to the 3rd Dynasty.	
This stratum is confined chiefly to the ground immediately under the wall, so that its thickness may be due in a measure to a bedding for the foot of the wall to rest upon.	3·0
Below this stratum the earth is nearly free from pottery.	
Traces of wall of small crude bricks, x × 11 × 8 c.m., three courses high, resting on the charcoal-discoloured stratum (third stratum); the walls are probably those of dwelling-houses of the period.	From 3·1 to 3·5
Charcoal-discoloured stratum at	3·5
Earth, dark owing to the presence of charcoal; occasional fragments of prehistoric coarse red and black-topped ware evenly distributed through it.	
Stratum of yellow clay 2 c.m. thick at	4·9
This stratum is harder than those above, and exhibits a slightly foliated structure. This is the old desert surface.	
Water, March 29th, 1899, at	5·7

NORTH ANGLE.

33. The Northern angle of the enclosure has been refaced, at some period, with small bricks 23 × 15

× 16 c.m. (9·0 × 5·9 × 6·3 ins.), held in position against the damaged face by mud mortar alone. No attempt at forming a bond between the new and old work has been made.

· At this angle, or rather in the N.W. wall, is a gateway, with a paving of rough sandstone blocks which formed the bed for the actual pavement of the temple. Under one of these rough blocks lay a small piece of red granite, similar to that of the inscribed block of Khasekhemui, and of the granite door sill on the N.E. side; this favours the supposition that the sandstone pavement of the door way was laid at the same time as, or subsequent to, the breaking up of the earlier work.

Within the enclosure, a wall of crude brick ran parallel to the N.E. enclosure wall, and probably joined one of the inner walls which are situated farther to the S.E. The part now standing is shown on the plan; the rest has been destroyed like all the work in this part of the site, owing to the denudation that has taken place.

FOUNDATION DEPOSIT.

34. In the angle formed by the S.W. face of this and the N.W. enclosure wall, what must be a foundation deposit was found. It rested on the crude brick pavement, the base of which is level, or nearly so, with foot of the walls; and was kept in the angle by a thin curved wall of 1·0 m. radius, built of crude bricks.

The deposit consisted of a mass of small earthenware vessels, the types of which are shown at the bottom of PL. LXVI. The bottom layer consisted entirely of the cup-shaped and dish-shaped vessels. On the top of these the skull of an ox or cow had been thrown, forehead down. Above this were more vessels of both dish and cup shapes, as well as a few of those of conical form. The topmost layer consisted, for the most part, of the bottle-shaped vases. All the vessels were unused. No order, except in a general way, had been observed in their arrangement; one or two large pieces of bowls had been put round the edge, where the mass exceeded the height of the curved retaining wall. The whole had been plastered over with mud to keep it in position.

No glazed plaques, or inscribed objects of any kind were found.

A pavement, such as once covered the rough sandstone blocks at the entrance, would have covered the deposit. No such pavement was, however, observed.

Fragments of prehistoric pottery (one decorated with comma shaped marks in the usual dull red) were found on the mud floor, or pavement, on which the deposit rested. This again shows the amount of disturbance of the lower strata that had taken place.

The N.W. side of the temple is bounded by a single thick wall. As already stated, the space between it and the circular Revetment has been denuded to a depth lower than the foot of the crude brick walls. No traces of any buildings were found here.

CHAPTER IV.

DATE OF THE MAIN DEPOSIT AND TEMPLE.

THE MAIN DEPOSIT.

35. THE walls of the group of rooms which are situated in the N.E. part of the temple, and under which the main deposit was mostly found, descend to a depth of 3·0 metres below the datum level, they are thus only from 30 c.m. to 50 c.m. above the charcoal-discoloured stratum.

The rectangular limestone block near which the inscribed palette of Narmer was found, and the stones, seemingly part of an enclosure wall round it, rest on the charcoal-discoloured stratum.

From this it seems clear that the main deposit must have been in this stratum. A piece of carved ivory, and a small ivory female figure, evidently part of this group of objects, were found under one of these deep founded walls, at a point 3·8 metres below datum level, during the second year's excavations. The palette of Narmer undoubtedly came from this stratum.

This leaves it uncertain whether these objects were actually in this stratum before the crude brick walls were built, or whether they were merely thrown into the foundations and built over. The presence of the two limestone squatting statues (PL. I.) as well as the human-headed door socket, all of which were certainly *in situ* below the later temple walls, as well as the great number of archaic objects, such as flint implements, spindle whorls, and inscribed clay sealings, which are found scattered throughout the charcoal-discoloured stratum, points to their having been in the ground at the time of the building of the later temple. On the other hand we have to account for the presence of an XVIIIth Dynasty scarab·which was found with part of the archaic objects of the main deposit by Mr. Quibell, and a fragment of pottery similar to that forming the foundation deposit in the N. angle of the temple enclosure, which was found under the wall near to where lay the ivory figure above mentioned. But, as before stated, as these walls descend to within less than 50 c.m. of the charcoal-discoloured stratum, it is possible that the scarab and the fragment of pottery fell into a trench dug in the archaic stratum to take the foot of the wall.

It is to such trench digging and general levelling that the wide distribution of some objects of the same period as the main deposit must be due : such as the presence of the stela of King Kha-sekhem, and the part of the base of the archaic statuette, which were found associated with New Kingdom pottery in one of the store rooms, and some fragments of a large ribbed porphyry vase with an inscribed lip (PL. LIX, 4, 5, 6, 7), which were found scattered all over the temple area. A fragment of one of the alabaster votive bowls, from the main deposit, with only the *ka* arms of the inscription showing, was found outside the enclosure wall about 48 metres from the granite door sill, or roughly 36 metres from the main deposit.

It is not likely that so few objects were scattered deliberately and that the rest were left together ; it is more probable that these objects were met with in the course of building operations, and that they were then thrown aside. If we assume this to have been the case, we must attribute the battering out of names and the damage which most of the archaic objects show, to an earlier period than the New Kingdom.

At the point where the fragment of votive bowl, just described, was found, the charcoal-discoloured stratum is 0·6 m. below the foot of the enclosure wall. Built against the lower courses of this wall is a pavement of crude brick similar to, and evidently part of, that nearer the Eastern angle of the temple, on which the flint points were found. This pavement extends outwards for a distance of 2·0 m. from the foot of the wall.

Above this pavement a stratum of charcoal and pottery has accumulated to a thickness of 20 c.m. It was in contact with the lower side of this, and 3·0 metres from the wall, or 1 metre beyond the edge of the pavement, that the inscribed fragment of alabaster lay.

In the accumulation itself part of a limestone mace-head was found, and above it was a fragment of Early Dynastic or prehistoric pottery.

DATE OF THE BRICK TEMPLE.

36. For determining the date of the crude brick temple we have unfortunately little to go upon. From the relation of the walls to one another, and from the fact of their being built of one size of brick, nearly the whole of these walls must be of one date. Under one of the walls of the group of rooms below which lay the main deposit a water-jar of the Middle Kingdom, or perhaps belonging to the early part of the New Kingdom, was found ; and among the archaic objects of the main deposit, not far from the limestone statue of Kha-sekhem and the great flint knives, Mr. Quibell found a green glazed scarab of undoubted New Kingdom type. The design consisted of the sign *neb*, below which was a sitting cynocephalus ape and a *shu* feather.

This may well have fallen in during the process of levelling the ground before the new walls were built, and need not have always been with the archaic objects.

Between the two enclosure walls on the N.E. side was found a model leg of an ox made of soft white paste, covered with green glaze, much bleached by the dampness of the soil.

This object is probably part of a foundation deposit ; but it was not *in situ*, and no pottery was found with it. Both sides had a cartouche written in black, now almost illegible, but most likely it is that of Amenhotep III.

Part of the pavement still left on the south eastern side of the temple, was made or repaired by fragments of earlier work, one of the sandstone slabs bearing the cartouche of Sebekhotep of the XIIIth dynasty on its under surface.

The crude brick walls seem to have been faced with sandstone, part of which is seen in contact with the southernmost pylon ; between which Mr. Quibell found a sandstone architrave with the cartouche of Thothmes III. As no dated objects were placed with the foundation deposit at the N. angle of the enclosure, and as the date of the pottery has not been determined, it does not afford much assistance. I do not see, however, why this pottery should be assigned to a period earlier than the XVIIIth Dynasty.

That kings of the VIth, XIIth and XIIIth Dynasties made gifts, and perhaps made certain constructions, is probable from objects of these dynasties being found; such as the stele of Pepy, a granite table of offerings with the cartouche of Usertesen I, and the paving slab with Sebekhotep's cartouche, already mentioned.

And further, we have a conspicuous absence of Middle Kingdom burials, while those of the Old and New are very numerous and important. This may be because the population was reduced at this period, and revived with the rise of the New Kingdom. As it is very improbable that this temple belongs to the Old Kingdom, this seems to point to the foundation of the temple at the later and more prosperous time of the New Kingdom. The sandstone cornice and polygonal column shown on PL. LXVII. may be part of the New Kingdom temple, or part of an earlier structure; but there is no evidence in favour of one of these dates more than the other. They were found at a considerable height, and above the floor which surrounds the sanctuary on the N.W. side.

CHAPTER V.

THE TOWN.

THE WALL.

37. THE remains of what was once the town of Hierakonpolis are enclosed by a crude brick wall, which, as may be seen from the plan, does not form a rectangular but a somewhat irregular figure: the line joining the north and south angles dividing the area into two nearly equal triangles having two of their sides bounded by walls meeting at right angles.

Unfortunately the wall has been in parts destroyed, or is now encumbered with modern huts, so that it could not be followed in its entire circumference.

On PL. LXXIII. the heavy black shows where the wall was actually examined, while the probable direction of the rest is drawn in outline only.

This town wall is built of small bricks, of about the same dimensions as those used in the houses (26 × 13 × 7 c.m., 10·2 × 5·1 × 2·8 ins.), but where it forms part of the outer enclosure of the temple on the S.W. side the bricks used are the same as those of the rest of the temple, 37 × 19 × 11 c.m. (14·6 × 7·5 × 4·3 ins.).

The general thickness varies but little from 6·0 metres where it is built of the small sized bricks, but where built of larger bricks it is but 3·0 metres thick. As the cultivation is close to the wall at this point, it is extremely unlikely that there was an outer wall of greater thickness, and traces of such a wall would surely have been preserved.

THE GATEWAYS.

38. Of the gateways which gave access to the town only two were found. One, which is in a very bad condition, the wall having been much broken at this point, is situated opposite to the north eastern entrance to the temple. Near it, and running at right angles to the town wall, are walls made of large crude bricks (37 × 19 × 11 c.m.), which seem to be part of some building forming an approach to the crude brick temple, and contemporary with it.

Another gateway is situated about two-thirds of the way along the wall towards the Northern angle.

The gateway itself, which is little more than 2·0 metres wide, had been paved originally with stone, part of which was found in situ resting on a mud bedding reddened in places by fire.

The stones forming the pavement rest on ground 1·7 m. below datum level, which is also the approximate depth of the foot of the wall.

Just outside the gateway on the north side, part of the base of a limestone statue had been placed upside down during some repairs of the pavement. Only the feet remain; they are coloured red as well as the plinth, which has had an additional coat of blue black put over the red. Judging by the work the statue seems to have belonged to the Old Kingdom.

2·6 metres in front of the gateway, and at a slightly lower level than the paved part, is a row of three stones roughly squared, resting on earth. Under them were a few pieces of rough red, and polished red, pottery of the prehistoric or early historic period.

ARCHAIC LIMESTONE STATUE.

39. The southernmost of the above stones was found to be a much mutilated limestone statue, of the most archaic and crude type, being very similar in technique to the limestone statues of Min found by Professor Petrie at Koptos. See PL. LVII.

The statue lay on its left side, with the upper part of the body towards the south. The head as well as the feet were wanting. Along the upper side, as it lay, was a row of shallow holes, evidently made by its being used as the lower socket to take the pivot of a door.

If the door had been placed as the position of the statue appears to suggest, in front of the gateway, it must have been the entrance to a projecting bastion with the approach parallel to the town wall. An assailant attempting an entrance would have presented his *shielded* side to the wall.

The statue is that of a man enveloped in a long cloak, descending from the left shoulder nearly to the knees, and leaving the right side of the chest bare. The left arm is held horizontally across the chest, while the right (which is disproportionately long and shapeless) is close to the side.

The right fist is pierced through horizontally, to hold staff or mace. The left leg is advanced; the knees are rudely indicated. There is no carving down the side, as is the case with some of the Min statues; all the marks seen are those of the tool, or mere meaningless scratches.

AGE OF THE TOWN WALL.

40. In the southern part of the site several walls were uncovered which seem to be contemporary with the town wall; they are thinner, but the bricks of which they are built are of the same small size. Their relation to the thick wall was not made out. As already mentioned there is a great confusion of walls at the southern angle of the temple enclosure.

The date of the town wall seems without much doubt to be early. The bricks of which it is built are of practically the same dimensions as those used in the construction of the houses situated within the town area; and these houses in some cases have been built against the inner face, proving that the wall is anterior to them in date. As all objects found on and under the floors of these houses, with a few exceptions that do not detract from the value of the evidence, belong to the first three Dynasties, it is clear that the wall must have been built at about the same date.

From the stratification it seems probable that as the town grew up it tended in time to encroach upon a holy place of high antiquity which is represented by the circular revetted mound within the temple.

As soon as the town had assumed sufficient importance it would be protected by a wall. This may have taken place at the end of the second or in the third dynasty. I see no reason for supposing the wall to be contemporary with the circular revetment; but it may very likely belong to the same period as

the squatting statues, though I am inclined to attribute it to a rather later date.

The use of the archaic statue as a door socket at one of the gateways, shows that the wall was kept in repair at a time when such objects had lost their sanctity; such repairs may have been made in the New Kingdom when the other archaic objects were broken or reused.

THE HOUSES OF THE OLD KINGDOM.

41. The whole of the area within the town walls appears to have been occupied by houses of the Old Kingdom; but, owing to the extent of the site, only those points were examined where the greater accumulation of earth gave hopes that the walls beneath had not been destroyed by the sebakhin.

On clearing these walls, the tops of which in some cases projected through the soil, it was seen that they formed groups of small rooms, the general orientation of which was the same as the part of the town wall nearest to which they were situated.

All the houses so far examined belong to the Old Kingdom, and practically all the objects found in them belong to the first three dynasties.

There is a noticeable exception that among the pottery scattered over the surface of the site, the bulk of which belongs to the Old Kingdom, there is a certain percentage of that incised ware which seems to be characteristic of the period between the Middle and the New Kingdoms.

Of objects that could be definitely ascribed to the Middle Kingdom, nothing was found; this statement is also true in a great measure with regard to objects of the New Kingdom.

The objects most frequently found in the houses were rough earthenware pots and pot stands (see bottom of PL. LXIX.), numerous fragments of diorite, quartz-crystal, and other hard stone vessels, numerous borers used in their manufacture, and a large number of clay sealings, some bearing the *ka* names of kings of the IInd and IIIrd Dynasties. In addition to these were numerous flint implements such as were found in the lower strata of the temple.

THE SEALINGS.

42. The clay sealings were very numerous, and widely distributed. Unfortunately they are in such a fragmentary condition that as a rule nothing can be made out of them.

Those best preserved are shown on PLS. LXX., LXXI.

What purpose these sealings served I am not sure. Many have the impression of papyrus, and some of cloth on them. One example has been put on a string, like the seal on a mediæval document ; others bear the impression of having been round a rod wrapped in papyrus or a small roll of papyrus. From this it seems probable that the majority have been the sealings on the papyrus strings tied over vases ; or, as the impression left on one suggests, on the top of a vase covered by a piece of linen tied over the mouth, much in the same way as a modern jam pot is closed ; while some may have been the sealings of bags or of the papyrus string fastening the bag, as is seen in some of the examples of the bag hieroglyphic *arf* or *g*.

The presence of inscribed seals in dwelling-houses is difficult to account for. They seem to have been invariably broken and thrown aside. It is incredible that they come from vessels containing offerings for the dead, stolen from the tombs, as they are distributed far too widely. I suggest, as an explanation, that they are the seals of the temple or town authorities, affixed to bags and vases containing either food, commodities, or materials required by workmen in their employ, issued as either rations or in payment for work done. Also, as the chief industry seems to have been, as far as can be determined, the manufacture of hard stone vessels, that such were the articles for which the payments were made, or in the manufacture of which the stores or materials issued were required.

SPINDLE WHORLS.

43. While dealing with inscribed objects of the archaic periods, we may here notice the frequent occurrence of limestone spindle whorls, many of which have marks rudely scratched upon them like those on pottery ; and two examples were found bearing hieroglyphic inscriptions *ur* and *hotep ref* respectively. Similar objects, also in some case inscribed, have been excavated at Hissarlik and in Crete.

These Egyptian spindle whorls seem too heavy for string making, as those used in modern and Roman times are quite light ; perhaps these were used as fly wheels for drills, rather than for spinning, and as many of archaic vessels, both earthenware and alabaster, have been repaired by drilling and binding the pieces together, this supposition is not improbable.

VASE GRINDER'S WORKSHOP.

44. The first group of houses examined was that marked 89, both on the plan of the town and on PL. LXVIII.

The walls are thin and their construction is careless, the angles deviating usually from right angles. In these respects they are but little better than modern Egyptian huts. The bricks are small, the usual dimensions for group 89 being 25 × 10 × 7·5 c.m. (10 × 4 × 3 ins.), and those used in the construction of the other houses vary but slightly from this. They were generally laid in courses of stretchers. The floors were of hard beaten earth, in some instances they are laid with crude bricks.

The circular structure in room 6, marked 10, is what the workmen described as a *shuneh* or place to contain fodder for domestic animals.

Room 12 of group 89 is a vase-grinder's workshop. The room itself is 2·6 × 2·1 metres (102 × 82 ins., 5 × 4 cubits). Access was gained to it by a passage with a door at the southern angle of the room. The sandstone socket of this door was found in place (marked 4 on the drawing PL. LXVIII. 1).

Round the room ran a bench of beaten earth 0·8 m. (2½ feet) above the floor. This bench projects considerably in the W. angle and to a lesser degree in the S. angle. The upper parts of these projections have cup-like hollows in which were vase borers, such as are shown on PL. LXII. That marked .1. was of chert. It stood with working surface upwards in the depression in the bench ; under it was a quantity of sand that had been used as the abrading material. On the top of the borer were two rough pieces of chert. Near to it (marked 2) was an oblong corn grinder. The borer marked 3 on the drawing was of diorite. Both sides had been used as working surfaces. Little or no sand was found in the socket or depression in the bench.

From the fact of the bench being 0·8 m. above the floor, it seems as if the workmen must have stood to their task ; the squatting position is, however, that represented on the reliefs, when the operation of vase making is represented.

All the pottery found in this group of houses was of well-known Old Kingdom types ; the rough earthenware pot-stands shown on PL. LXIX. are, however, not very common.

In the earth, from the level of the foot of the walls, up to and on the present ground surface, numerous fragments of hard stone vases and bowls were found.

D

Similar fragments, as well as the vase borers scattered all over the site, afford evidence of the extent of this vase-making industry.

Several clay seals, some inscribed, were found in this group of houses; they occurred generally on, or slightly higher than, the floors. In some cases where they were found at higher levels, they owe their change of position to sebakhin digging, or to disturbance of the soil at a more ancient date. Among the objects of special interest that came from this group of rooms is a rough-baked clay cylinder seal, bearing unintelligible marks upon it, which was found level with the foot of one of the walls. The group also yielded several rectangular flint blades; these occurred generally on the floors or in the talus heaped against the outside of the walls. A few fragments of flint knives of the hafted type were also found.

In the stratum just below the walls of room 5 a wide-mouthed jar of well known late prehistoric type was found; this jar appears to have been used for a burial, but no bones were found in it; from the way in which the wall of the room is built over it, it does not seem to have been a house burial, but to have been unwittingly covered over by the builders.

1·2 metres below the foot of the walls, or 3·9 below datum level, part of a forked lance of dark flint, and some fragments of prehistoric pottery, were discovered.

In the same room nearly 1·0 metre below the foot of the walls was a small copper rod of square section.

Near the top of the walls of this group part of a clay doll belonging to the period between the Middle and New Kingdoms was found.

The following section, made in room 1, group 89, shows the stratification met with in the town area.

—	Below Datum Level.
	Metres.
Top of walls	0·7
Fragments of Old Kingdom pottery and stone vessels down to	2·3
Talus of rubbish in contact with the walls, consisting of earth blackened by charcoal, and containing a few fragments of Old Kingdom pottery.	
Foot of walls at . . . . resting on stratum of dark loam containing coarse pottery and charcoal, becoming cleaner towards the lower part.	2·7
Whitish sand with occasional fragments of coarse red prehistoric pottery.	
Water level, February 1st, 1899, at	4·8

HOUSES 145 AND 172.

45. A group of houses, 145, 172, has been built against the town wall. These houses, like all the rest uncovered, belong to the Old Kingdom, and the presence of houses built of similar bricks to the town wall, and in contact with it, seem to prove that it is at least as early as they are themselves.

In this group of houses were found numerous fragments of inscribed sealings, Old Kingdom pottery, limestone spindle whorls, and fragments of stone vessels, among which was part of a cylindrical alabaster vase with a rope pattern below the rim. Also here was a piece of black incised ware of the prehistoric period, an archaic cylinder seal of dark baked clay inscribed with unintelligible marks PL. LXIII. 5, and the flint hoe shown on PL. LX. 13, which lay on its flat side 0·6 m. below the foot of one of the walls.

HOUSES 205, 180, 211.

46. The houses of group 205 and 180 contained the usual pottery of the Old Kingdom, as well as several fragments of clay sealings, some of which bore the ka name of Seneferu, neb-maat.

Near this are some walls, to which reference has already been made, as forming part of an approach to the temple, and in all probability of the same date, as the bricks of which they are built have the same dimensions, 37 × 18 × 11 c.m.

Under these walls and in the archaic strata were several flint knives of the hafted type, Old Kingdom pottery, and a limestone spindle whorl with hotep-ref rudely incised, see PL. LXXI.

In group 211 a number of Old Kingdom pots had been placed together in the angle of the passage on the south side. The principal types are shown on PL. LXIX.

Fragments of seals, some inscribed, rectangular flint implements, and a limestone spindle whorl inscribed wr (PL. LXIII. 1) were found.

HOUSES GROUP 144.

47. This group of houses is situated at the northern part of the town. In this were found the usual Old Kingdom pottery, flint sickle teeth, and flint knives; also a small vase with pointed base, made of green glaze, and a plaque bearing a hawk in low relief. The body of the plaque is composed of a white

friable paste similar to that of the green glazed objects from the main deposit.

The plaque and the vase are shown on PL. LXIII. The earthenware vase shown next to the green glazed one came from near where the main deposit was found, and at the same level; these vases are here shown together for the sake of comparison.

Besides these objects were two vase borers, one the same shape as the largest of the group shown on PL. LXII. 5; and the other like the medium sized one of the same group.

A large piece of quartz crystal, roughly chipped to shape, ready for grinding and polishing, came from this group of rooms, PL. LXII. 4. The borer shown on the top of it in the plate was not so found; it is shown thus to give an idea of the probable mode of manufacture.

HOUSE 168.

48. A little north of the group just described is another set of dwellings, marked 168 on the plan. The group consists of a series of rooms opening into a passage 1·8 m. wide, running at right angles to the town wall. These rooms must have had entrances higher than the present height of the walls (about 30 c.m.), as the actual doorways were not found.

The most westerly room is the largest; it is divided into two parts by a low wall. In a room adjoining it on the north side is a "shuna," or circular structure, like that already described as occurring in group 89.

The room next to the first is nearly square; and next to this again, is another square room, but larger and divided into two parts by a low thin wall. Still further towards the town wall, separated by a recess or blind passage 2·0 m. long by 0·6 m. wide, are two rectangular rooms 2·4 m. by 2·0 m. and 2·6 by 2·0 respectively.

These rooms contained the same kind of objects as all the rest, but a greater number of rectangular flint blades were scattered about the floors in this group than in any of the others examined, most coming from room No. 1. Here, as elsewhere, were found pottery of the Old Kingdom, a few green glaze barrel-shaped beads, one made of a bright green stone, a human tooth, several inscribed fragments of clay sealings, and a small ivory bangle.

Among the clay sealings one was found in a remarkably good state of preservation in the most westerly room, in the angle formed by the partition wall and the low cross-wall. Its original shape had been a cylinder whose height is less than its breadth. It bore the impression of having been round a roll of papyrus or papyrus knot. Unfortunately it had been broken in half and the other part was not recovered.

The impression of a cylinder runs round the side and over both ends, the inscription reading KHA NETER AKHT KHENU. (LXX. 3.)

Besides the Old Kingdom pottery a piece of the dark ware with incised cross lines belonging to the period from the Middle to the New Kingdom was found.

Still further to the northern angle of the town wall some walls are shown on the plan. These appear to have formed part of a large room, but they have been so destroyed by sebakhin that they stand now only about 20 c.m. above their foot at the highest point, while the greater part has been removed altogether. That they belong to the same period as the rest of the houses is evident from the size of the bricks, and from the nature of the few objects, such as pottery, that were recovered. Nothing of interest except a few fragments of pottery was found.

CHAPTER VI.

THE FORT.

BY SOMERS CLARKE, F.S.A.

49. THIS building lies on the desert edge, but very little removed from the cultivated ground, and at the mouth of a valley which runs into the western desert. In plan it is rectangular, with the entrance towards the cultivated land. An outer wall has been built 2·34 m. thick, standing in advance of the inner and chief wall, which is 4·87 m. thick. There is a space of 2·23 m. between the walls. The outer wall was lower than the inner.

The entrance is formed in a sort of bastion, or tower-like projection, and is sufficiently circuitous to make it impossible for any body of persons to rush through quickly. There is not evidence that any other entrance existed. The outer wall follows the plan of the projecting bastion. It is, however, so much ruined at this point that it is impossible to say definitely whether the doorway was in the long face towards the N.E., or in the short return face towards the N.W. There are indications which suggest that it may have been in the return face, and this arrangement would have made it most easy to defend.

If there were stairs of ascent to the wall top, and we cannot suppose there were not, these must have been of wood, and placed in the slits on either side of the entrance. All traces of them have now vanished.

In the entrance can still be seen remains of panelling in the brickwork.

Whilst the surface of the outer wall was plain, that of the inner wall, facing into the narrow space of 2·23 m., was built in panels. The walls are entirely of crude brick, and were plastered and whitened.

50. The bricks are of moderate size. They vary between 25 × 12 × 9·0 c.m. (9·8 × 4·7 × 3·5 ins.), and 30 × 14 × 7·0 c.m. (11·8 × 5·5 × 2·8 ins.). They are laid with little attention to bond. The face is nearly always neatly arranged with alternate courses of headers and stretchers ; but within the bricks are all laid headers, i.e., their length is across the thickness of the wall. Sometimes the bricks are not laid flat, and we find a course of bricks on edge, but laid without method.

The courses of bricks are horizontal, and not laid (as in the great walls at El Kab) in curves convex and concave to the horizon. There is no timber bond built into the walls, nor are there courses of halfa grass or reeds laid in the mortar.

The south west wall remains unbroken, and stands to a height of some 8·0 m. or 9·0 m. above the plain. The walls near the gateway are also of about the same height, and it is probable they have not lost more than 1·0 m. The building corresponds in most respects with the rectangular brick fort at Abydos, known as the Shunet ez Zebib, which is, however, considerably larger.

CHAPTER VII.

THE CEMETERY.

51. THE large prehistoric cemetery which extends from the fort to the drainage line, shown on the S.E. end of the map, has been so plundered and destroyed that hardly a tomb has escaped. In the first season's excavations Mr. Quibell, after examining some of these plundered tombs, confined himself chiefly to that part of the cemetery near to, and west of, the fort, as this part had escaped the almost total destruction that had overtaken the more easterly portion.

52. During the second season's work one of the workmen, who was a resident in the neighbourhood, reported that there were walls with signs of paint on them at the extreme South East of the cemetery.

These walls, on being cleared of sand, showed a bricklined prehistoric tomb decorated with coloured drawings, very similar in design to those seen on the decorated pottery of the period. The tomb had been plundered, the walls in places showing marks of the hoe, and all objects of value were removed.

As far as I could ascertain, several large flint knives had been found ; but the natives, as is usual in such cases, were either unwilling or unable to state when or by whom. Judging by the amount of sand which had drifted in I should think that it must have been rifled two or three years previous to its examination by me in 1899. See PL. LXVII.

The tomb consists of a chamber about 4·5 × 2·0 × 1·5 metres (15 × 6½ × 5 feet) with the upper parts of the walls flush with the desert surface ; as may be seen from the transverse section, it was built in an excavation in the desert whose sides slope ⅘. After building these walls sand was filled in behind; and this loose sand is shown in the section by the dots being spaced wider than that of the untouched desert.

The walls consist of small crude bricks which vary considerably in size, their average dimensions are 23 × 11·5 × 9 c.m. (9 × 4½ × 3½ ins.). All the lower courses were built of rows of headers on their flats ; the second course from the top is however built of stretchers on their flats. The walls had a batter of ⅘.

The mud of which the bricks are made contains numerous fragments of prehistoric ash-jars. The mud used as mortar is as a rule more yellow and sandy than that from which the bricks themselves are made ; it has also set rather harder.

The tomb is divided into two equal parts by a low cross-wall abutting on the middle point of the N.E. wall.

The height of the walls does not seem to have been much more than the highest standing wall, as the upper parts when undamaged turned inwards slightly, as if close to the roof. The roofing must have been of wood as no signs of a vaulted or corbelled roof of any kind were seen ; and several of the graves in the immediate neighbourhood have remains of the round wooden logs or roofing beams showing in the sides of the excavation.

The floor was paved with crude bricks of the same dimensions as those of the walls.

The whole of the brickwork, including the floor,

had been plastered over with a layer of mud mortar about 5 mm. ($\frac{1}{4}$ inch) thick ; this, in turn, when on the walls, had been covered with a coat of yellow ochre or whitewash.

53. On wall B (PL. LXVII.) there was no sign of paint ; it may have been left simply plastered, but of this I am not certain as the surface is much damaged.

C and D were also plain.

E had a white ground and a dado 27 c.m. (10$\frac{1}{2}$ ins.) high of blue-black, bounded on the upper part by a line of red ochre 2 c.m. wide. On the white ground were traces of figures in red ochre.

F, ground white, blue-black dado 27 c.m. high ; bounded on the top by red ochre line 2 c.m. wide, like wall E.

G, ground white. No signs of painting. Probably never decorated. Blue-black dado 35 c.m. (14 ins.) high bounded by red line 2 c.m. wide.

The wall A, A, has been decorated all over. At the lower part is a dado of blue-black, which varies somewhat from 27 c.m. (10$\frac{1}{2}$ ins.) in height, owing to the rough way in which it has been executed. The upper part of the dado is bounded like the rest by a red ochre line 2 c.m. wide, painted over the blue-black.

The surface of the wall above the dado has been coloured a light buff with yellow ochre, perhaps with the intention of representing the desert. On this buff ground hunting scenes, combats, and large boats are portrayed with rude skill, the animals especially being very spirited in execution. No definite order seems to have been attempted. It cannot be said that the lower part represents the river bank, and the upper part the desert ; but the scenes seem to have been put where there was room for them, after the larger designs, such as the boats, had been drawn.

The generality of incidents depicted are the hunting and trapping of wild animals, encounters with lions and men, while boats of various sizes and designs represent the more peaceful side of life.

It should be noticed that none of these boats show the propelling oars such as are shown on the pottery. There is an example of a prehistoric boat on one of the rocks near El Kab, where the hull is carefully shown by hammering all over the surface, but the oars are mere hurried scratches, as if put in by another hand ; so that the propelling oars were not invariably shown.

The long and generally round-ended steering oars are always shown ; and several examples of what may be meant for the anchor hanging from the prow.

The dress of the figures should be noted ; the leopard skin which later became part of the ceremonial dress of the priests is interesting on this account, as well as the *uas* sceptres held by some of the men.

The curious rectangular figures seen on some of the decorated pots, seem to be intended for these leopards' skins spread out and drying in the sun.

On wall F there had been a representation of a procession of men, which probably extended to wall E ; unfortunately the surface of both walls, especially E, had been so much damaged that except part of the procession on F, nothing could be made out.

The execution of the drawing on wall F is a great advance on that on wall A, and shows a distinct trace of what later developed into the Egyptian style.

54. The colours used are, for the ground, either yellow ochre, or white. The blacks are a blue-black, and do not seem to be pounded charcoal. All the boats, except one, have been painted white, over which a wash of bright green, granular in structure, probably pounded malachite, had been put. The exception is a boat with a high prow and comparatively low stern, which is painted blue-black.

The outline of the figures was drawn first in red ochre ; the white of the dresses has in many instances overlapped this outline. The eyes were put in with a thick pasty lump of white ; the pupil being represented by a blue-black spot on this.

All the decorated surfaces had suffered much from exposure, and direct damage. It was only by repeated tracing and copying, in different lights, that many parts of the scheme of decoration could be recovered.

In many places also the artist had rubbed out his red outline, thus reddening the yellow surface before re-drawing his design ; when the surface was damaged this added to the difficulty of copying.

As already stated the tomb had been plundered of all objects of value. Many of the ash-jars, and other pottery, had been left ; these are shown on the plan, the letters and numbers appended refer to the plates of pottery published in *Naqada and Ballas*.

Besides the pottery were found part of a forked lance flint shown on PL. LXIV., and a small vase of hard limestone or chert. Of the body there remained no trace except a few fragments of bone in the southern division of the tomb, which may have been part of the skeleton.

55. Near the decorated tomb was another with a brick lining, plastered over with mud, but no colour had been used. This had been plundered, nothing remaining but a few coarse jars.

At a short distance to the south of the decorated tomb there was one with the southern part divided off into two small compartments by low walls. The pots and other offerings which these compartments held had all been stolen, only a few fragments of pottery being left.

The rest of the graves were mere rough rectangular excavations in the hard desert sand varying in depth from 2·0 m. to 0·5 m. The roofs had in many instances been made of wood as the remains of the ends of the beams were found in some cases. In one grave the roof was supported by wooden columns the holes into which their bases fitted still remaining ; this grave is shown on PL. LXVII. Nearly all had been robbed, and most of those that had escaped contained little except pottery.

The general orientation is very roughly north and south ; but no special care seems to have been taken, as some of the examples deviate very considerably from this line, and a few are east and west, these latter being small rather shapeless and shallow excavations.

From the graves that were more or less untouched the objects shown on PL. LXIV. were recovered. They belong to types already known except the bowl 1, which resembles the pottery found in the Pan-Graves at Hu : but there is no doubt that this example belongs to the prehistoric and not to the later period, as all the objects associated with it were prehistoric, and the grave itself appears to have been untouched.

The spheroidal spindle whorls shown on the same plate should be contrasted with those of hemispherical shape from the town and temple areas, belonging to the early dynastic period.

Besides the main prehistoric cemetery, close to the cultivation, there is another smaller one at the mouth of the valley south of the rock-cut tombs of the New Kingdom and extending some way up it.

Two or three isolated graves, containing nothing but the skeleton and a few rough pots, were found half way between the sandstone cliffs and the southern end of the cemetery.

The tomb shown at the bottom of PL. LXVIII. is situated at about two-thirds of the way towards the fort from the decorated tomb, and near to a group of tombs of later date than the Old Kingdom. The tomb appears to belong to the late prehistoric or early historic period, but it may be later.

56. DIMENSIONS AND DETAILS OF UNBAKED MUD-BRICKS. HIERAKONPOLIS, 1899.

Dimensions in C.m.	In Inches.	Situation.	Date.	Remarks.
37 × 19 × 11	14·5 × 7·5 × 4·3	Temple	XVIII Dyn. (?)	Average dimensions.
37 × 19 × 11	14·5 × 7·5 × 4·3	Temple. "Skewed wall"	XVIII Dyn. (?)	Foot of wall is 0·2 m. above rough stone-work.
37 × 19 × 11	14·5 × 7·5 × 4·3	Outer enclosure wall. S.W.	XVIII Dyn. (?)	At this point the outer wall of the temple takes the place of the town wall proper.
26·5 × 12 × 8	10·4 × 4·7 × 3·1	N. end of prehistoric cemetery	Early or Old Kingdom	See plan, and sketch on Pl. lxviii
26 × 13 × 9	10·2 × 5·1 × 3·5	Fort. Outer wall	Later than prehistoric	The Fort is built over the prehistoric cemetery.
26 × 13 × 8	10·2 × 5·1 × 3·1	Most easterly mastaba	Old Kingdom	On west side at the mastaba, and the interior bricks same dimensions.
26 × 13 × 8	10·2 × 5·1 × 3·1	Middle mastaba	Old Kingdom	Mean of three measurements.
26 × 12·5 × 8	10·2 × 4·9 × 3·1	West mastaba	Old Kingdom	The fort is built over the prehistoric cemetery, and may be contemporary with the mastaba, as the orientation is approximately the same.
26 × 13 × 7	10·2 × 5·1 × 2·7	House 186	IInd to IVth Dynasty	Measurement of several bricks, but not from one specimen. Breadth varies between 6 and 8 c.m.
25·5 × 10·5 × 6	10·0 × 4·1 × 2·3	House 186	IInd to IVth Dynasty	In wall built of stretchers.
? × 9 × 9 / 23 × 11·5 × 8	? × 3·5 × 3·5 / 9 × 4·5 × 3·1	Decorated tomb	Prehistoric	Vary considerably in dimensions; these were from inner face of walls.
? × 12 × 9 / 21·5 × 10·5 × 6	? × 4·7 × 3·5 / 8·4 × 4·1 × 2·3	Near site	Modern Arab	For the sake of comparison; modern bricks vary considerably.

DESCRIPTION OF THE DISCOVERIES.

By J. E. QUIBELL.

CHAPTER VIII.

INTRODUCTORY.

57. DURING the winter of 1897–8 excavations were conducted for the Egyptian Research Account at Kom el Ahmar, a large part of the cost being borne by Mr. Jesse Haworth, Mr. Somers Clarke, and the late Mr. J. J. Tylor.

The share of the objects found that was brought to England was exhibited at University College in July, 1898. Mr. Green continued the digging in the winter of 1898–9, and a second exhibition was held in the following summer.

A volume of plates was issued in 1900, with notes by Prof. Petrie. The present volume contains the plates depicting the objects found in the second season, with some plates omitted from the first publication ; and the description of the site in detail by Mr. Green, with the account of the discoveries by the present writer. The delay in publication that has taken place is regretted by none so much as the authors. The first cause was the necessity of my going to Berlin for the summer of 1898, and thence in the autumn to Gizeh. The work connected with the exhibition, and with the making into plates of the photographs and drawings, fell upon Mr. Green's shoulders alone.

58. From this delay it has come about that a considerable amount of comment on the monuments of Hierakonpolis has already been published by various savants : Maspero, Naville, Foucart, Capart, Max Müller, Spiegelberg and others, besides the notes of Prof. Petrie, issued with the first volume. A good bibliography may be found in Capart's paper "La fête de frapper les Anou" (*Revue de l'histoire des Religions*, Tom. XLII.).

To the questions raised and the identifications suggested by these scholars I have seldom alluded, for the reason that the detail of excavation furnished no material by which such questions might be resolved.

Besh may be a king's name, or may mean "rebel" : Khasekhemui may be the same king as Khasekhem, or may be his successor ; Narmer may be identical with the 9th king of the Abydos list, or, as Petrie has shown reasons for believing, may belong to the first part of the 1st Dynasty or be even earlier.

In each case the latter of the two alternatives seems to me the more probable, but there was not evidence on the site to decide these points one way or another. So I have confined myself in this account to the endeavour to give the observations made during the digging as shortly and clearly as possible.

59. For the drawings reproduced in the first volume we were indebted to Mr. Peers, to Mr. Somers Clarke, who often came over from El Kab to help us, and especially to Miss A. A. Pirie. Miss Murray has kindly helped us, by drawings and otherwise, in England ; and Mr. Mace has spent much trouble especially over the ivory. Lastly to Prof. Petrie, the director of the Research Account, are due my thanks for help given ungrudgingly on all occasions. Such help he has always given in furtherance of those excavations with which I have been connected ; and it is only in obedience to his wish that this help has not been earlier and more fully acknowledged.

CHAPTER IX.

KOM EL AHMAR.

60. KOM EL AHMAR is the name given to the large cemetery on the W. side of the river from El Kab : it applies more properly to the mound of red pottery of no great size or prominence which lies E. of the fort. The name does not distinguish the site from the numerous other ancient mounds of potsherds in Egypt, also called Kom el Ahmar, "the red mound" ; so the undoubted Greek name Hierakonpolis has been taken as the title of this book.

The fort is still a considerable structure with

massive walls of unbaked brick, panelled on the outside, a thinner outer wall, and a large gateway; a building of the same type as the Shûnet ez Zebîb at Abydos.

North and south along the edge of the fields the desert is seen to be much dug over by *sebakh* diggers and dealers. Hundreds of archaic graves lie open, and fragments of pottery and stone vases strew the soil; all the damage has been done within the last ten years.

Close to the fort on the W. is the low hill in which are the two well-known decorated tombs of the Old Kingdom; and further to the W., at a distance of twenty minutes' walk up the dry stream bed, is another series of sandstone hills, in one of which can be seen the row of entrances to the group of XVIIIth Dynasty tombs.

Over all the ground for two miles N. and S. of the fort, some search was made; but the results, though not devoid of interest, showed that the ravages of the Theban dealers had been more extensive than was expected, and that but little of the cemetery had been left.

61. The fort was first examined to see if its nature and date could readily be ascertained; but here the *sebakhin* have actually dug to a greater depth than the foot of the wall; so that, except at the S. end where there is a mass of fallen brickwork, no remains of the same date as the wall were expected. Some archaic graves lie under the walls, and in the same place are some of the same tiny trenches with branches at right angles, such as were found beneath an archaic village at Ballas.

They are about 10 cm. in width and depth, and may have served for the footing of wattle-and-daub walls. The mud of which the bricks are made contains fragments of archaic pottery, and this is the only evidence of their date that was found.

62. To the E. of the fort is the low red mound which is sometimes called specially Kom el Ahmar.

It consists almost entirely of fragments of pottery of the common Old Kingdom types, mixed with a few pieces of the red and black archaic ware. These lie heaped over a group of buildings with bee-hive domes, and small square doors high up on the S. side, no doubt granaries.

The fragments seem to have been thrown out from a kiln, but the granaries are of unburnt brick, and show no trace of fire. The two dug out were filled with clean sand. The bedding of the layers of potsherds shows that the granaries have not been built

in pits dug in the mound, but that the broken pottery has been heaped round them. They must then belong to the early Old Kingdom, and be among the oldest of non-funerary monuments. There was originally a group of twelve or more of these buildings, but all but three or four have been carried away by *sebakhin*.

63. Immediately to the north of the fort, and of this mound, is an area which once contained archaic tombs, but is now completely dug out. Then comes a group of three small mounds of brickwork which were clearly mastabas.

Of these the largest, that to the W., when dug out, displayed a plan of some interest. It is a stairway tomb with a small chamber below ground to the S. The space between the two surrounding walls is divided into chambers by half-partition walls, but these chambers contained nothing but filling, and in the stairway and chamber below were fragments of alabaster cylinder-jars, and of the common coarse pots of the Old Kingdom.

Of the other two mastabas one had a central well instead of a stairway; both contained fragments of diorite and limestone vases, but no inscribed object, nor anything which would differentiate them from any other mastaba : and the outer sides of the mass of brick were so cut away by *sebakhin* that it was impossible to trace them.

One point, however, of great interest rewarded our work here. The stairway of the E. mastaba appeared to be not quite in the centre of the building; there might, it seemed, be another well hidden by the untouched brickwork; so a trench was driven right through the centre of the structure from the N. side, and under the mastaba, and on the untouched surface of the desert was found a plaque of green glaze like that shown in PL. XVIII. 2. (The photograph is taken from another plaque found afterwards below the temple.)

The plaque is oblong, slightly convex in front, with a projection behind pierced with a hole for wiring, and is exactly like the famous plaques from the step pyramid of Saqqara, which are now at Berlin. The position shows beyond doubt that the plaque is not later than the Old Kingdom.

64. Further to the N. are other small patches of cemetery : the graves are not found on the lowest ground, but on the low black mounds of clay, which form in many places in Upper Egypt a noticeable feature of the strip of desert that borders on the cultivation. These mounds appear to be made of

E

Nile mud, but are really of considerable geologic age. They were found by the archaic people very convenient for digging tombs; and the traveller by rail, between Luxor and Edfu, may see many mounds that have been so utilised.

In one of these mounds was a group of tombs of a type new to me. The graves were 1·5 to 2·0 m. long, 1·2 m. broad, and 70 c.m. deep, and lined with brickwork. At the N. end of the tomb two tiny cells, 20 c.m. square and 30 c.m. deep, were bricked off: in two cases these were occupied by coarse vases, and in one of these there were traces of grain. The body was in the regular contracted position, head S., face W. The grave was covered with a sandstone slab.

In one tomb were fragments of flat alabaster dishes; in another a rectangular slate palette, a smooth pebble, and an alabaster cylinder-jar; in a third, part of a wooden coffin; while in a tomb situated in this group, but in which the body faced E., was one of the thick wooden cylinders, about 2 c.m. long and of the same diameter, similar to the well-known black stone cylinders of the earliest times.

This was our limit to the N. Beyond it comes a mile or more of desert in which no tombs have been found, and then the pyramid of Kelh.

South of the fort is a watercourse leading up to the round hill containing XVIIIth Dynasty tombs.

65. Near this hill, a little to the south, is a large tract of smooth desert, on which small fragments of archaic pottery may be picked up. As no tombs lay open we expected to find here an untouched cemetery, but were disappointed. Not a single tomb was discovered. The potsherds were scattered over acres of ground; but below them, save in a few circular patches, the desert had not been touched. In these patches, which were about 2 m. in diameter, a layer of ashes and charcoal about 2 c.m. in depth showed that for some purpose large fires had been lighted there. The ashes were covered by about 5 c.m. of gravel and sand, washed down from the hills.

At other points, further to the S., pottery was scattered over the desert in much greater quantities, again without graves to account for it, but on a soil that had been disturbed. This was, at first, difficult to account for, but an explanation of at least one such spot was given me by a *fellah*. One of the low mounds of black clay, mentioned above, had stood there, containing many archaic graves; the whole mound had been carried away as *sebakh*, and the pottery from the graves left behind.

This explanation will, no doubt, suffice for some places, but not for all. Some villages must have existed here, and all the brick walls have been carried away later by *sebakhin*.

In this southern part there are also patches containing archaic tombs, but only the very poorest were left untouched. There is also a small group of late Middle Kingdom (?) tombs near to the fort; all robbed.

In the archaic tombs that were opened, most of the features observed in the cemetery of Naqada recurred. There was one clear case (No. 225) of mutilated burial, a covering of skin and mat above the separated burial being untouched. The lining of tombs with mats, and the use of skins to cover the bodies, was common here. In one tomb the skeleton of a dwarf was found; in another were painted clay models of flint knives; in another two fine copper chisels and an adze-blade. The fine tomb decorated in the style of the painted Naqada pots, was not found till the second season.

66. Altogether, the results of the work on the cemetery, though by no means devoid of interest, would by themselves have hardly repaid the season's work. I therefore began upon the mound within the cultivation, which at first had not seemed promising, but where a remarkable series of monuments was soon to be unearthed. This *kom* is the town of Hierakonpolis. It is a rectangular rise, hardly deserving the name of a mound, for it is but slightly higher than the surrounding fields; watercourses are cut through it by the fellahin; the boundary walls can be barely distinguished; very soon, unless care be taken, it will slip into cultivation and disappear.

But early in the century it must have been of a considerable height. Old peasants remember the walls 6 metres high; some part of the temple, too, was then standing, and it is only within the last thirty years that the stones have been taken to Esneh to build a factory.

Formerly the town must have stood on the very edge of the desert, if not entirely within it; but with the rise of level of the country, the cultivation has crept up the gentle slope of the dry stream-bed, and now there is a belt of watered land, 300 m. wide, between the town and the desert.

The greater part of the line of the town wall can still be traced: inside it, to the N., is a part covered with a thick layer of pottery thrown from the *sebakh* diggers' sieves. Here, too, is a line of modern huts; but most of the mound is covered with the *aqûl* plant, and a coarse grass on which the goats continually feed. In the S.W. of the square, another wall, very clearly visible, cuts off one corner from the rest of the town. Within this enclosure the soil was generally smoother and at a lower level than elsewhere, except where at one point a rise of 2 m. showed where a brick building had stood. Two or three battered blocks of granite were also visible, and the base of a sandstone column. In the middle of it stood two Arab huts, which were afterwards bought and demolished; the granite blocks of Kha-sekhemui were found under them, one serving as a corner-stone of the hut. A watercourse ran across the site fed by a *shaduf*, which worked in an ancient well. This enclosure was clearly the temple.

It was in this small area that the remainder of the season's work was concentrated, and in it were found the three groups of objects, those of the gold-headed hawk, the copper statue, and the great deposit of slates, ivories, &c., on which the importance of the results depends.

67. The gold hawk was found in the first week of the work; it chanced that we began to dig over the group of five chambers (v. PL. LXXII.) at the N. of the site; and, while clearing out the first of the chambers, found in the centre of it a small bricklined pit, the top of which, at a lower level than the base of the surrounding walls, was covered by a roughly-hewn basalt slab (v. PL. XLII.). When this was raised the pit was seen to be filled with moist earth. As this was cleared there came into view a hawk of thin copper plate, with head and plumes of gold. Underneath the bill of the bird stood a statuette of a king: both faced south. Below the flat base of the hawk was a hollow cylindrical rod of thin metal, and the whole was supported on a stand of red pottery: the rod ran down the centre of this, and was embedded in a vase of rough pottery at the lower end (v. PL. XLVII.). At the bottom of the little pit lay four small vases of earthenware, and the objects sketched in PL. XLIII., an alabaster vase, two small maces, a fire-drill cap (?) in limestone, and an *uas* sign of green glaze. Some beads of green glaze, stone and gold foil, also lay on the floor of the pit, and others were scattered through the filling; they had probably served as a necklace for the hawk.

The whole pit was filled with the moist and heavy earth. As it was cleared from the top, the gold plumes were first found, standing in place with one long gold nail projecting forwards from a hole in the middle line. Below this was the circlet standing

I c.m. above the head. These were all in perfect preservation, unaltered except by the red patina of old gold. But the thin plates of copper had become extremely brittle, decayed by the dampness of the soil. No particle of the wood core on which they must have been nailed had been spared: so directly the upper part of the body had been uncovered and the form disclosed, long cracks appeared and the thin shell soon broke into scores of pieces.

The head and plumes have been mounted and can now be seen at Cairo; the restoration of the body has proved a more difficult matter, and is not yet finished.

The pit was in the centre of the brick chamber, but below it, the covering slab being on the same level as the foot of the walls. The sand surrounding it was very clean, and in it were found many fragments of pottery of the earlier archaic period, and part of one of the forked flint lances (type of XXIV. 17). Among the potsherds were pieces of the "red and black" ware, the coarse and the "polished red," but no fragment of the later types, such as were found in the royal tomb of Naqada or at Abydos.

It seems from the circumstances of the find, that the hawk was buried under the floor at the time these five chambers were built. Probably it was buried definitely, not merely put away in a safe place to be taken out again for certain festivals; for, if this had been the case, we should hardly suppose that the small ceremonial objects (maces and *uas* sign) would be buried with it.

68. In the next chamber to the E. of the gold hawk there was nothing of importance, and the sand below it showed no sign of disturbance; but below the next to this the sand was not clean, and on digging further we found, at the depth of 1 m. below the base of the wall, a singular spectacle (v. PL. XLVII.). The two legs of a life-size copper statue lay side by side. Below and beyond the thighs, the face appeared, and the left fore-arm stood up on one side. Over the feet of the figure lay, head downwards, a lion of red pottery, about 40 c.m. high, and by its side, nearly touching the lion's muzzle, was a green stone statue of a seated figure, the head of which was missing.

Here again the soil was moist, and though the lion and the stone statue were untouched, the metal was corroded and very brittle, and the green rust had fastened the surfaces together. For the lion, see PLS. XLIV. and XLV.; for the stone statue, PL. XLI.

E 2

When the two legs of the statue had been removed, the torso below was seen to be incomplete, the hips being missing. On the chest, and adhering to it by the green corrosion, lay a crumpled sheet of copper with an embossed inscription of Pepy I. (PL. XLV.).

The statue was taken up to the tomb in which we lived, and an attempt made to clean out the hollow trunk. It was then found that this contained a smaller complete statue of the same technique as the larger, and divided in the same way into three pieces, body and two legs. This could not be conveniently removed with the means at our disposal, and the torso was brought down to Gizeh, with the small statue still enclosed in it. At the Museum both figures were very skilfully restored by M. Barsanti, and the photographs show the statues as they now stand at the Museum. Some fragments of the plate, with the embossed titles of Pepy, have also certain eye-shaped signs, of which I did not at Hierakonpolis see the meaning. M. Barsanti pointed out that they are the ends of the bows on which the king is often represented as standing, and Dr. Borchardt showed us that the small statue and the large one probably formed a single group of the king with one of his sons.

This proved to be the case: the arrangement of the bows gave the approximate breadth of the inscribed plate, and showed that it had covered the common base of the two statues.

The back of the head and the hips of the king are missing; doubtless they were formed of some other material than copper: traces of gilt plaster remain on one thigh.

The technique of both statues is the same: they are formed of plates of copper, joined together by rows of nails (not rivets), placed close together. These must have been driven into a core of wood. The seams run down the inside of the arms and legs. The sides of the trunk and the forearms are made separately, and fastened in the same manner at the elbows. The core of wood must have been extremely rotten when the statues were taken to pieces, or the nails would have been bent and the plates damaged. But this observation does not help the dating, for the *termites*, or "white ants," in Egypt now sometimes render a village uninhabitable by eating every particle of wood in it.

69. The lion is of a porous reddish pottery, with a bright red polished surface. It is of the same material and technique as some of the fragments of statues found below the temple of Koptos, and as the Osiris statuettes from the Ramesseum and Medinet Habu. In condition it was perfect, except that it was saturated with salt.

There is no inscription on it; but in the form of the face, and the treatment of whiskers and mane, it closely resembles the lions on an alabaster table of offerings from Saqqara, attributed to the early Old Kingdom.

70. The green stone statue (PL. XLI.) shows the king wearing the crown of Upper Egypt, and a large robe folded across the chest and falling nearly to the ankles; this is the robe used in the Sed festival. Scratched on the base, in front of the feet, is the Horus name of the king, *Kha-sekhem*, and round the sides of the base are rudely-scratched figures of dead bodies lying on a field of battle. These inscriptions make us attribute the statue to the early Old Kingdom, though the style of the figure would have led to a much later date. Unlike the lion or the Pepy statue, this object is somewhat battered, and the right side of the head was never found, though a wide search was made.

Of these three objects one is of the time of Pepy; of the others, one and probably both are of much earlier date. The copper statues had been taken to pieces, and their wooden cores removed, the sheathing of the base torn off, and crushed together, and the whole packed in a compact manner so that it could be buried in a small hole.

The hole was in the centre of the chamber, and the discoloured sand did not extend beneath the walls.

Therefore the objects were buried after the walls were built, and most probably very soon after.

The good state of preservation of the copper statues seems to show that, though they had become obsolete, they were still thought worthy of some respect, and were so saved from the melting-pot.

This group was buried in the sand without any surrounding walls or covering slab.

71. The third of the groups was still more remarkable than the last, and contained a great number of objects, all of them, apparently, of the earliest historical period.

They, too, lay at a low level, below all the existing walls of the temple, at a point on the E. side of the temple area, and to the south of the set of five chambers mentioned above. Here there was a small rise of about 2 metres in the ground, the ancient walls having been for some reason much less denuded here than elsewhere. When this mound was cleared a group of chambers was disclosed, the contents of which were not of importance; but as the walls did not rest on undisturbed sand we went down deeper, and just below the level of the walls began to come upon scattered objects of the archaic period.

It chanced that the first objects found were those close to and under the N. wall of the middle room. There were two sharp-edged stone maces, a flint knife, and a vase with a large conical seal of yellow clay. These, with other objects, lay all together, and the wall had to be undermined to obtain them. Another pit was made on the N. side of the wall, and more than twenty objects, all of archaic types, were found lying together; a green glaze monkey, a large quartz mace, and some pieces of inscribed ivory.

Two other trenches skirting this same group of rooms, and approaching from the N. and E., ran into similar groups of archaic objects. In the middle of these different groups the objects were really heaped one on another: at one point limestone maces lay in scores, and, stained by the clay, looked much like a heap of potatoes. There was also a great heap made up entirely of objects in ivory, chiefly statuettes.

We at last realised that we had found a great heap of archaic objects, not distributed in separate chambers, as Amélineau's finds in the royal tombs made us expect, but carelessly thrown together.

The heap was approached from every side till its boundaries were known, and the objects were gradually removed. This was a month's work, and for more than half this time we were working with penknife and steel ruler, instead of adze and basket, extricating the delicate objects from the sandy clay in which they were embedded.

It is impossible to give a detailed plan of so confused and close packed a heap of objects; and as the order in which they were taken out was largely accidental, it will be simpler to give a general account of their relative positions, following this by a complete list of all the objects found in the group, but leaving details of measurement, &c., to the catalogue in the plates.

This will involve some repetition, but the fault is hard to avoid.

72. The best point to begin will be from one of the largest objects, the flat slab of stone which lay near the S.E. verge of the group. It was apparently the base of a statue, or something of the kind, 1 m. 26 long, 80 c.m. wide, and 25 c.m. thick; the top of it sunk, and leaving a ledge 26 c.m. wide round

the margin. It lay E. and W. Nothing stood on this base: its surface was rather rough, and bore no inscription, so I left it *in situ*. Close by it, to the N., W., and S., and on the same level, were parts of a wall or pavement of squared limestone blocks, six in a double row to the N., a single row of four to the W., and three to the S. Those to the N. were in contact with the stone slab, the others were a metre away; and in the space between to the W. lay the great slate palette (PL. XXIX.). Under the stones lay a lot of coarse potsherds and a fragment of bone. This masonry, and a bit of wall made of small bricks which was found a little further to the south, formed the only fragments of building connected with the great deposit; for, as has been already said, the system of brick walls shown on the plan lie at a higher level, and have nothing to do with the archaic objects.

Immediately to the S. and E. of the stone slab lay a mass of objects, more than seventy in number, heaped together with no discernible order; they included a model bedstead (?) of limestone, broken maces, stone vases, and objects in glaze. Further to the E. was the smaller decorated slate palette, and under it another palette (plain) and a fine flint knife; still further to the E., about four metres away, stood the large granite vase with the inscription of Kha-sekhem. To the N. of the stone slab the objects lay still more thickly. Here was the heap of ivory: it lay in a mass about 2 m. long (N. and S.), and not quite so broad, a confused heap of statuettes, cylinders, and wands; some had been broken before being placed there, but most could have been removed complete had not the ivory been in so lamentable a state. The ground was moist, the mixture of sand and clay was heavy and rather tough; the long tap roots of the camel-plant ran through the mass; more than once I observed that a root had found its way through the layers of ivory, and pierced through the length of a statuette, splitting it up as it grew.

There was a good deal of various salts in the ground, and a crystalline layer had sometimes formed between the layers of ivory; more often it had been deposited round the outer surface, covering the object with a tough, dirty-white mask: and often one piece would be fastened to another by the same material. The ivory itself was of various degrees of consistency; sometimes a mere yellow paste, or a little heap of grains or needles, lying in a hollow in the clay; sometimes just so well preserved that we could affirm, "This must have been a statuette about a foot long," but so rotten that, as we looked, it fell into dust; sometimes it had more consistency, splitting up, much like boiled fish, into curved plates or sheaths which slid upon one another. Often the trunk of a figure could be got out entire, but the neck fell away into dust; and nearly always the outer surface was much decayed, so that all the finer modelling was lost.

Day after day we sat in this hole, scraping away the earth, and trying to disentangle the objects one from another; for they lay in every possible position, each piece in contact with five or six others, interlocking as a handful of matches will, when shaken together and thrown down upon a table.

The process of cleaning was continued at the house; with vinegar and dilute hydrochloric acid the lime and salt incrustations were removed, and then some of the pieces of ivory were soaked in gelatine, melted stearine or beeswax. But most of the consolidation was done subsequently by soaking in boiling wax in London.

The results were disappointing; much was, indeed, saved, and I do not see that much more could have been done by any method yet suggested. But it was lamentable to see how much lay there just too far decayed for preservation. Had but the site been drier, scores of ivory statuettes of fine workmanship, and dating from the earliest periods, would have enriched our museums.

73. By the side of the ivory, to the E. of it, and N. of the stone slab, was a lot of pottery with rough alabaster dishes, and a heap of pear-shaped maces. This group, too, lay in a line N. and S. The pottery consisted of vase-stands, 20 to 30 c.m. high, made of a very coarse ware, with an oblong cist, like those found in tombs, and two of the large hemispherical bowls, called by the natives *magurs*. One of these was nearly filled with a collection of small objects of alabaster, green glaze and quartz, and its mouth was covered by a bowl of red and black pottery.

Further to the N.E. the succession of finds continued right under the wall. They included a pot with raised cord pattern round the shoulder (similar to the vases so numerous in the Abydos royal tombs, but smaller), more maces and scorpions, a heap of more than 1400 spiral green beads, the two great inscribed maces, and the limestone statue of Khasekhem.

Here, too, was found the only object which might be considered not to belong to the archaic period—a scarab of glaze, with the signs ⟷, the baboon,

and ⌠. This would, undoubtedly, be dated to a later period, perhaps to the Saite, and it is puzzling to account for its presence as a solitary stranger in this collection of older objects.

There are several possibilities. The sides of the hole stood above us several feet as we were working, and on the ground-level above there were undoubtedly chips of late pottery. Even Roman remains were found not far away, and it might be said that the scarab fell into the hole without being observed, was trodden into the moist clay close to the early stuff, and afterwards dug out again. But this is in the highest degree unlikely; the danger of such accidents is so well known, that the slightest sound of falling sand will make the observer look up, and anyone approaching the edge of a pit that is being cleared is always hurried back. The scarab may be much more ancient than we think; it may belong to the period when the archaic objects were buried, or it may have been introduced at a later period by some accident.

No explanation is quite satisfactory. The fact remains that this one scarab was found, a solitary late object among many hundreds undoubtedly archaic.

74. The following catalogue gives details omitted in the preceding paragraphs; the same general order from S. to N. is followed, and groups of objects which lay close together are so mentioned.

Catalogue of great deposit.

In S.W. verge.

A stone slab, with sunk top, perhaps the base of a statue or a shrine.

S. of this, and going from W. to E.

> Limestone mace.
> Glaze scorpion with inlaid eyes.
> Flat alabaster plate (Type XXXIV. 3, 4, 5).
> Two scorpions of glaze.
> Limestone mace.
> Hotep sign of gold foil.
> 3 small vases of pottery (one XXXV. 14).
> An alabaster cylinder-vase, containing two quartz tablets.
> An ivory statuette.
> Mace in shape of double ram head.
> Monkey in green glaze.
> Another holding a vase.
> The jaw of some animal undetermined, perhaps a dog.
> Bottle-shaped vase of black serpentine.
> Next to it, the tail of a scorpion of rock crystal

(PL. XVIII. 16). The body of this scorpion was never found.

An eye of lapis lazuli and obsidian (?) (length, 1 c.m.). This had fallen, most probably, from an ivory figure (*cf.* PL. VIII. 6); and the fact that no more eyes were found, supports the view that the statuettes had been much damaged before they were buried.

Mace-head of hard yellow limestone (6 c.m. long).

Mace-head of rock crystal.

Mace-head of porphyry.

Large mace-head, of sharp-edged type.

Stone vase with handles, rough.

Model of a bedstead (?) of limestone and breccia; 4 pieces, 2 of which lay together, PL. XXVIA.

Bottle of green glaze.

Bowl of green glaze.

Half of a monkey in green glaze.

Small bowl of limestone.

Green glaze vase with handles.

A model boat of serpentine.

Cylindrical vase of pottery, grey-pink colour, plain, no markings round neck; similar to those from a royal tomb of Naqada.

Small squatting figure of limestone.

The smaller of the decorated slate palettes.

Another palette, plain.

Fine flint knife (PL. XXV., centre of top line).

A small vase (PL. XXXV. 14).

The last four objects lay close together; the decorated slate above the other, and this on the knife.

Coarse stand of pottery.

Further E. (3 metres from the stone slab).

Another piece of the stone couch (?) (PL. XXVIA.).

Compound vase (quintuple).

Mace-head of porphyry.

Large sharp-edged mace.

Small alabaster dish, flat.

Small statue.

Jawbone of a small animal.

Still further E., beyond the limits of the main deposit, and 4 metres from the stone slab.

Granite vase of Kha-sekhem; it was full of earth, in which were potsherds of coarse archaic ware, and of red pebble-polished

pottery, a green glaze monkey, and a bit of a grooved porphyry vase. This last must have come from a magnificent vase, similar in shape and size to that on PL. XXXVI. 4, but adorned with vertical fluting.

Fragments of it were found widely scattered, not only in the great deposit, but elsewhere in the temple.

Outside the vase, but close to it, were

A fragment from the rim of a large porphyry vase, with an inscription in relief (PL. XVIII. 21); most probably this is from the same vase as the piece last mentioned.

Small dome-shaped block of alabaster.

Green glaze hippopotamus.

Green glaze vase on stand.

Square plaque of ivory with a hole in the centre.

Rod of glazed quartz.

More fragments of a large porphyry vase, one inscribed.

Fragment of limestone, probably from the great mace, PL. XXVIB.

S. of this last group, and still underneath the brick wall, were

16 limestone mace-heads; with them inscribed mace of PL. XXVA.

Pottery vase, XXXV. 15.

Scarab of green glaze, apparently late.

Two green glaze mace-heads like XX. 6.

Below these were numerous green glaze beads, mostly long cylinders and barrels; also a rectangular ivory plaque; small figure of captive (faience); ivory spoon; and fragments of alabaster vessels, stands of coarse pottery, and a large sharp-edged mace. Just within the chamber were

Dummy limestone vase with scorpions in relief (PL. XXXIII. 1).

Red and black pottery vase.

A large jar (to contain fat, etc.) like those found at Abydos.

An alabaster mace-head.

Small spherical vase of green glaze.

A little further to the S., just under the level of the S. wall of the chamber, were

The fragment of an alabaster bowl with inscription of Kha-sekhem, PL. XXXVII. 3.

Boat-shaped dish of serpentine, like that of
PL. XXI. 1, but with no snakes below.
Two pottery bowls with stands combined, like
XXXV. 6, but taller.

Near these were

Another group of plain limestone maces.
The fragments of the very fine carved mace,
PL. XXVIB.
Parts of two very large flint knives, PL. III.
Small seated statuette of basalt.
Small pot of green glaze XVIII. 18.
Head of a monkey, green glaze.
Two spherical flint nodules.
An alabaster bowl.
A serpentine mace in form of four bulls' heads.
Small limestone lion.
Steatite frog.
Alabaster frog.
Pottery scorpion with a peg below, and a hole
pierced in the peg.
Limestone monkey, 18 c.m. high.
Limestone statuette of squatting human figure,
15 c.m. high.
Small animal of limestone (? dog).
Fragment of limestone, with mark of scorpion
and arms as on the alabaster bowls, PL.
XXXIV. 3.

At the N.E. end of the chamber, under the wall,
came the following series.

Small green glaze vase with handles.
Sharp-edged mace
Pear-shaped mace.
Large sharp-edged mace.
Flat alabaster dish.
Black incised bowl.
Coarse cylindrical alabaster vase.
Flint knife.
A piece of copper plate crumpled into a mass
as big as a fist: small nails could be seen
sticking in it.
Some spiral beads of glaze.
Two of the pieces of quartz like vase handles.
Scorpion.
Vase with seal of yellow clay.
Fragment of a green glaze vase on stand (open
work).
Haematite scorpion, tail broken.
Vase and stand, green glaze.

Quartz bar, broken at one end, hole pierced at
the other, XXIV. 5.
Cylindrical green glaze bead surmounted by
two apes facing one another.
Coarse pottery stand.

N. of the wall were

An ape in green glaze.
Cylindrical alabaster jar.
Mace.
Long pottery jar.
Horus amulet, limestone.
Large sharp-edged mace, broken.
Ivory rod.
Ivory cylinder, human figures incised.
Ivory rod with carving, PL. VI. 7.
Pottery *magur*.
Piece of quartz, shape of half a cylinder.
Some pieces of ivory.
Monkey of green glaze.
Cylindrical alabaster vase.
Serpentine vase with the *set* sign in relief.
Round-bottomed vase of alabaster.
Four maces.
Cup-shaped mace.
Half of a flint knife.

The following objects were found in the mass of
ivory statuettes, wands, &c.

A vase of gneiss (shape PL. XXXII. 6), broken.
Small round steatite jar, flat-bottomed with
horizontally pierced handles.
Fragment of a similar jar of steatite.
Numerous fragments of alabaster dishes, two
inscribed like PL. XXXIV. 3.
Two alabaster bowls, as PL. XXXIV. 5.
A fragment of coarse black pottery, with incised
criss-cross lines.

Most of the ivory lay to the N. of the stone
slab, and W. of the pottery, alabaster, and maces.
Owing to the bad condition in which it was found, it
is impossible to give the numbers of the different
pieces. The best are figured in the PLS. VII.–XVI.,
and all the classes of ivory objects are there represented, except that of the larger statuettes about
40 c.m. high. No one of these was well preserved.
This list does not show all the archaic objects found
in the temple; but those not here given were found
at some little distance from the main group.
The two limestone statues, with the small objects

found behind them, may well really belong to this series: they may have been buried at the same time, and in the same circumstances; but there was a small empty space between them, while in the great deposit itself there was hardly a foot of ground that did not contain some monument.

To the polished syenite vase of Pl. XXXVII. the same remarks apply, and the revetment must also belong to the earliest period.

CHAPTER XII.

THE AGE OF THE REMAINS.

75. THE bare facts of the relative positions of the objects as found have been given: an attempt must now be made to give a date to the making of the monuments themselves, and to the time at which they were buried.

The main objects to be considered are the revetment, the brick walls, and the three deposits.

The revetment is undoubtedly very early. The clean sand within it, containing nothing but archaic potsherds and flints, the depth of its foundation, and the fact that similar work of naturally cleft stones was found in other parts of the temple site, but only at the lowest level, all make this point clear.

76. The brick walls offer more difficulty: they are of one character and size of bricks, and appear to be all of one period. Two pieces of evidence as to this period were found, but they were contradictory.

The first was given by a pile of fragments of Middle Kingdom water-jars, heaped against the outer face of the town wall to the S.W. near the water-channel. This would lead one to suppose that the walls were built during, or before, the Middle Empire.

But between two of the walls there was a scattered foundation-deposit of Thothmes III. And the pylon, as it was covered with blocks bearing his name, was probably an original construction of the same king. The question which it is desirable to answer is, to what extent Thothmes rebuilt the temple, and especially whether it is to him, or to another earlier king, that the walls over the archaic finds are to be attributed.

The dark clay below the foundation of the walls might have given the answer, but though it was often searched for fragments of distinctive XIIth Dynasty pottery, none were ever found. All the sherds were of Old Kingdom types.

77. The golden-headed hawk is certainly connected in some way with the chamber under which it was found. It was buried in a carefully-bricked pit, square with the chamber, the top of the pit being just below the level of the foot of the walls. It is possible, if not very likely, that the god was kept here for safety, and dug up at intervals for special ceremonies; but the small objects with it, so much like those in foundation deposits, suggest that the burial was intended to be permanent, and that this hawk was the actual idol of the temple, honourably buried when it was superseded by a more magnificent successor.

If this be so, the hawk was buried at the time the N. part of the temple was built.

As the body of the hawk and its stand are made of thin copper plates attached by nails, a rare method of construction, and as, a few yards away, another chamber of the same building, and buried at the same level, a statue of Pepy of the same construction was found, it is attractive to assume that hawk and statue are of the same date. There is, at any rate, no difficulty in supposing that the hawk is as early as the VIth Dynasty or earlier.

In the second group two objects, the statues of Pepy and Kha-sekhem, are dated by their inscriptions, and the lion also is probably of Old Kingdom work. All three were buried after the walls were built, and at the same time. And this time must have been long after the reign of Pepy.

78. Of the main deposit three statements may be made; it is not a tomb; it consists of temple furniture and nothing else; and the objects are all of one general period.

The suggestion that it was a royal tomb has been made more than once, and with some plausibility. The slate palettes, which are glorified examples of the palettes of the Naqada tombs, the flint knives, the ruder stone bowls, are all what we might expect to find in a royal tomb. But the idea cannot be maintained. The presence of monuments of at least three different kings, the absence of the great stores of pots usual in the Abydos graves, the almost total absence of brick work, and the careless way in which the different objects were heaped together, are surely conclusive.

The objects, too, were buried intentionally, not lost to sight by an accidental accumulation of dust. This is shown by the vase filled with small objects, by the large vases being covered with rough pottery lids, and by the fact that the ivory was found in a long heap, just as if it had been buried in a trench.

F

And many of them were broken before they were buried. This was observed in several cases, and the fact that only one eye was found among all the ivory statuettes, so many of which had once had inlaid eyes, shows in how bad a state they were before they were laid aside.

We are forced then to suppose that, as they do not come from tombs, all these objects are pieces of temple furniture, difficult as it is to imagine to what use they could be put.

But the representations of the Sed festival at Soleb show that the maces, which are so numerous at Hierakonpolis, were used in the ceremonies, and the fine slate palettes may well have been used for the daily dressing of the god.

79. The conclusion that all the objects are of the same general period is drawn from the objects themselves. The ivories, for example, are of a uniform style throughout ; no one would think of dividing them by their style into an earlier and a later class. Now the small cylinder of Narmer is certainly early ; the figures of men with pointed beard and peaked cap are like the men on the ivory combs of Naqada ; the ships with double cabins are the same that we see on the painted pottery ; the elephants (VI. 6) are drawn by a man who knew elephants well, just as they are on the early statue from Koptos, not as on the Una stele ; the decoration of lines of animals is the same as on the Pitt-Rivers knife (Naqada, Pl. LXXVII.) ; the bulls' feet are exactly like those from the Abydos royal tombs. Much of the alabaster, too, bears inscriptions in early signs known on the rude Abydos steles ; the maces are common in archaic tombs. In fact, most of the objects are clearly of the archaic period, and there is no reason to doubt the earliness of the rest (the case of the scarab, discussed above, being excepted).

The great group may then be unhesitatingly attributed to the earliest historical period.

There was, however, a doubt as to whether the whole of it was buried under the same circumstances. The ivories and other small objects seemed to me to have been buried in trenches dug to receive them ; but the stone slab with some building round it (the first object mentioned in the list of sect. 74), had been built into its position, and the two limestone statues (one in frontispiece), and the human-headed socket, were clearly in their original position at the entrance of the early temple.

It is because of this apparent difference in the circumstances of burying that I have hesitated to class these two statues in the third group, near to it though they were.

But there is nothing incompatible in the two facts. If we suppose that the level of the temple was deliberately raised, that the heavier monuments of the older building that were not needed for the new were left *in situ*, and that the smaller objects were buried in trenches made while the earthing-up was going on, we have a very natural explanation of the observed facts.

80. Lastly, the main deposit must have been buried at the same time as the group with the copper statue of Pepy, for each contains a statue of Khasekhem, and the two statues, though of different material, are similar in pose, dress and general style, and bear identical inscriptions. The inscriptions may, indeed, well have been made by the same workman. It must be remembered, too, that the Pepy stele, though at a rather higher level than the archaic objects, lies among them in plan.

The simplest explanation then seems to be that the revetted mound was part of the earliest shrine. Khasekhemui built another temple, still at a low level, to which additions were made by both Pepy I. and Pepy II.

At some later period a reconstruction was decided on ; and, as the level of the town would by that time have risen, and the houses near would overtop the temple, the site was filled in and the floor of the new temple was raised to the top of the revetment. In these new foundations all the objects we found were buried with the exception of the granite door-jambs of Khasekhemui, which were hauled up and re-used. At the same time one piece of the water-channel from the old well-head was built into the foundation of the wall.

But there is one difficulty in this account. If it was not till the XVIIIth or XIIth Dynasty that all the archaic remains were buried, how comes it that among all the hundreds of pieces, not one that was not archaic should be found ? Some pot or bead definitely dateable to the Middle Kingdom would surely have strayed into the collection. And the later we suppose the burial to be, the more difficult it is to explain the uniformity of date of the find. It would be much simpler to believe that all the archaic objects were buried as early, say, as the IVth Dynasty. But for one archaic object, the green statue of Khasekhem, we know that this cannot be the case.

Another explanation is possible. There were two statues of Khasekhem, one of limestone, the other of green schist. Owing to exposure to damp or other causes, the limestone figure soon decayed and was buried at an early period with a lot of other archaic temple furniture. The green statue lasted several centuries more, but at last got broken and was buried with the Pepy at a second rebuilding.

This hypothesis (due to Von Bissing) removes one difficulty, but it brings up the level of the Old Kingdom temple to the top of the revetment and causes another difficulty over the gold nails.

Three of these nails, indistinguishable from those found in the gold hawk's head, were found at the lowest level at a point S. of the revetment. They were either from the hawk or from some object like it. Therefore we shall have to put the hawk into the period before this hypothetical Old Kingdom reconstruction. And this does not seem likely.

It must be further remembered that in the main deposit was found a mass of crumpled copper plate just like that from the base of the statue. This increases the probability that the statue of Pepy and the main deposit were buried at one and the same time.

[NOTE.—The system of pegging with small metal nails, and the use of copper foil, undoubtedly belong to prehistoric times; hence neither these gold nails nor the copper sheet are of any value as shewing a date equal to that of the hawk or the Pepy statue. —W. M. F. P.]

CHAPTER XIII.

DESCRIPTION OF THE PLATES.

THE following description of plates is in consecutive order, irrespective of whether they appear in Vols. I. or II., as many persons may wish to bind the whole as one work.

PLS. I. and II. 1. A life-size statue in white limestone, height, 0·85 m., 33 ins. The right knee, broken off in PL. II., has now been put back as in PL. I. The statue represents a king (?) kneeling on the left knee with the left foot under the body and the right knee raised. The left foot forms part of the base, which is small, and does not project beyond the body. The face is curious: the eyes are prominent; the beard, which is broken, was wide and not of the narrow and short form of later time; the whiskers are marked in slight relief, as in later statues, so as to look like a band supporting the

beard. The short square-bottomed wig is divided in two by a parting at the top, from which lines 2 c.m. apart lead downwards; these divisions then narrow suddenly to curls 10 c.m. long.

The only dress is a belt 3 c.m. wide with a small kilt or tassel in front; the kilt is square ended now, but is somewhat broken.

The general outlines are round; the hands are puffy, with little detail. The surface was never polished, and is covered with scratched lines from the original working. The limestone is not of good quality, and by long exposure to damp had become so soft and friable that, had it not been for great care in packing, the statue could hardly have been brought to Cairo. For this care we are indebted to Dr. Schweinfurth, who was staying at El Kab soon after the statue was found. He procured a quantity of the cheap unsized paper used by the traders in the country markets, soaked it sheet by sheet in water and applied it to the surface of the statue, pressing it well on with the fingers; when one layer had nearly dried another was applied, and so on until the whole was covered with a mask of paper an inch thick. With this protection the statue travelled well.

This method of packing is of great use in Egypt for such objects as cracked vases and fragile skulls; the paper dries so rapidly that there is no fear of its becoming mouldy.

Another statue of the same kind was found with this one, but in so bad a condition that it could not be brought away. The two were erect, 2 m. apart, on the E. side of the temple, near the main deposit of archaic objects, and on the same level with them (v. PL. LXXII.).

2. Fragment of a flat limestone slab, on scale of ¼. From the style of the two signs it is supposed to be archaic, but no conclusion can be drawn from the position in which it was found. This was on the W. side of the temple, in a much disturbed part, and the objects near it were a pot of XIXth Dynasty (?) shape, a bowl of XIIth Dynasty, a potsherd from a large vase of later archaic shape, and a fragment of a stone window which might have been of any date.

3. Granite door jamb of Kha-sekhemui, now at Cairo (height 1·55 m., width 1·20, thickness 0·60) The photograph shows the edge only. One side is also inscribed, but the inscription has been bruised out and is illegible. The block is not complete, the lower edge being broken and showing by its curved outline and the wedge marks that a millstone has been cut out of it.

F 2

Two other large blocks were found close by; one bore, like this, the king's name, the other was a fragment of a list of names of countries (v. PL. XXIII.).

These blocks lay near the surface, on the level of the top of the revetment, and close to it on the S. side.

PL. III. 1, 2. Large ceremonial flint knives, formed from natural layers of flint chipped around the edges. The larger is over 30 ins. long.

3, 4. Two views of a door-socket of hard dark stone, found with a rough jamb of limestone (1 m. × 0·4 × 0·15) still standing on it.

A human face projects in front, representing an enemy crushed under the door: his arms are roughly indicated on the top of the block. The hole on the top is for the pivot. This was found just to the W. of the two seated statues; the door socket stood in the passage way (0·9 m. wide), between two fragments of brick wall (1·10 thick); these were much decayed, but one could see that they were made of much smaller bricks than the rest of the buildings, and such small bricks are, at El Kab and Kom el Ahmar, typical of Old Kingdom structures. The walls were also skew to those of later date, i.e. rather E. and W. than N.W. and S.E. Twenty centimetres above the level of the door socket, and resting partly on the bit of ancient door wall and partly on the loose earth, was a horizontal ring of rough cylindrical vases laid on their sides, with the base of one in the mouth of the next. The diameter of the circle was 2·3 m. In the middle of this ring were two coarse pots of the *magur* type, and of these one contained five archaic models in green glaze, a jar of flour (?) (XVIII. 13), a box with rounded top, a vase on a stand (like XX. 11), a bird, and a baboon. The pots forming the ring were wheel-made. Near and below the door socket were found fragments of later archaic pottery, a scorpion of green glaze, a bit of gold foil, some barrel-shaped glazed beads and fragments of ivory.

From the low level at which it lay, its position behind the pair of statues, the archaic objects remaining near, and the patch of ancient wall against which it stood, it seems that this door socket must have belonged to the archaic temple.

It should be noted that this object was about on the level of the base of the revetment, while the granite doorway of Khasekhemui was near the top.

PL. IV. A sketch of the revetment taken from the top of the U-shaped wall on its south side (v. PL. LXXII.). In the middle, low down, is a drum-shaped block of limestone, sunk at the top like the base of a statue. On the sides, partly resting on the circular stone, are two roughly-built walls whose finished faces are on the inside. They were not completely cleared when this sketch was made.

The staff in the foreground is 2 m. long.

The revetment consists of a single layer of rough sandstone slabs covering a bank of sand. The stones are now so fastened together by salt that they will bear the weight of a man, but this cannot have been the case when the structure was built. The slope of the revetment is 45°, and the height at the best-preserved part 2·30 m., (7½ ft.,) or 24 courses of stone. It runs right under the brick walls. The sand inside is clean, and contains nothing but a few sherds of the early red and black pottery, and fragments of fine early flints.

PL. V. 1. Head of very soft limestone; the projecting lips are like those of the large statue of PLS. I. and II.; eyes were inlaid; no marks of eye paint; the head was from a small squatting statue, the greater part of which fell to pieces.

2, 3. An ivory head of European rather than Semitic or Egyptian type.

4. Boat of ivory, with a small cabin, in which sits the owner wrapped in a large cloak.

5. Three boats in relief: the two cabins joined by a bridge are as in the paintings on the Naqada pottery.

PL. VI. 1–5. Photographs of the two heads of the last plate.

6. Part of a tusk with birds and animals in relief; a drawing with the curved surfaces developed is on PL. XVI. The elephant in the second row is shown walking on the hills, like that on the statue of Min from Koptos. The next rows show water-birds, and (?) hyænas. At the base, women with long wigs, and long and elaborate dresses, carry some curved objects in their hands. The best preserved figure seems to have the ear of a cow.

7. From a plaster cast of a palette-shaped piece of ivory. The decoration shows human figures (? captives) in groups of three.

PLS. VII.–XVI. show in drawings and photographs the best preserved of the ivory carvings.

PL. VII. 1 and 6 show the peculiar dress, explained by Naville as a sheath (*Recueil*, vol. XXII.).

2 shows the tall pointed cap, known also from a decorated comb at Naqada.

3 is a small head with a new kind of cap.

5 shows the ordinary Egyptian kilt.

PL. VIII. 7. Headless figure in a large cloak. Other kinds of heavy cloaks are shown in IX. 3 and 4.

PL. IX. 1, 2. Two views of a female figure fully draped and with elaborate hair-dressing ; the feet are not represented.

3. Same as X. 8. This is the cloak of the *Sed* festival. The figure was probably pegged on to a support.

7 and 8 give two varieties of women's wigs.

PL. X. Photographs of figures given in other plates.

PL. XI. 1, 2, 3. Three views of a bow-legged, deformed female figure ; it was made of two pieces of ivory pegged together. The head is very short from back to front.

4, 5, 6. Figure of a Libyan, probably from a chair or some such article. There is a square tenon above to secure it in place.

PL. XII. 1. Part of a cylinder, developed. In the top register a wild ox (?), below cranes, then some antelopes, and at the bottom pelicans.

4. An ivory mace, the only one found ; the second sketch shows the development of the design, which is that of captives tied together by the neck, their arms being fastened behind them. The existence of this piece as a link between the ivories and the other monuments should be noted.

5. A small ivory figure, one of four found ; they probably stood back to back, served as supports for a cup, and represented captive foreigners. The figure was much encrusted with tough lime. The top of the head is flat, and has a hole in it for pegging. The square-bottomed kilt is similar to that of the limestone statue of PL. II.

6. Another of the four figures, apparently an Asiatic.

7. A lap-eared dog wearing a collar.

8. In relief ; ibex or goats, some birds and gazelles.

9. Handle of a spoon, with some animal in the round ; see spoon in *Naqada* PL. LXI.

PL. XIII. Two similar objects, arms of a chair, ends of the bearing poles of a palanquin or the like. [Dancers' wands, as in *Deshasheh*, PL. XII.—F. P.] The peculiar appearance of the reliefs is due to the outermost layer having often fallen away.

No. 1 retains the tenon, with hole for a peg by which it was fastened ; the animals represented are not easy to name ; in 1 there are oxen, hyænas, and some water-birds ; and in 2 some antelopes, an animal

I do not recognise, and hares. Both ends of No 2 are flat ; the figures of men in relief on top and bottom are barely to be seen.

PL. XIV. This carved tusk was found complete, but in such bad condition that its top broke before it could be removed. Much of the outer surface flaked away before the drawing could be made, and the whole tusk has since perished by an accident. The rows of birds and ibex occurs on several other pieces ; but the architectural ornament above with the heads of animals suspended over the doors is peculiar. The bucrania recalls the painted skulls found by Petrie in the so-called "pan graves" at Hû (*Diospolis Parva*, pp. 26, 46).

PL. XV. These cylinders are hollow ; no evidence of their use was obtained, but it may be that several of them were joined together on a metal stem to form the handle of a mace.

The sketches are on a scale of $\frac{1}{4}$ and the developed designs $\frac{3}{4}$. The subject in three here illustrated, and in several others that were not drawn, is the familiar one of the Egyptian smiting with his mace a captive whose hands are tied behind his back. The figures are incised, the drawing rough and unfinished.

3. A scene of singing.

5. Unrecognisable animals (? cats).

6. The sign of the pendant arms, frequent in these early inscriptions, is shown in more detail than elsewhere.

7. The smallest cylinder, and the most interesting. In the centre is the name of the king of the large palette, Narmer (?). The fish sign is shown with human arms holding a large staff ; while before and behind it, in three registers, kneel captives with their hands tied behind their backs. Above the king's name is the protecting vulture, and facing it is the hawk deity of Nekhen. This cylinder, then, is doubtless of the time of Narmer, and this fact is a guide to the dating of the rest.

PL. XVI. 1, 2. A wand of ivory carved on both sides ; it is notched like a sickle on the lower edge, on the back is a snake in high relief. The designs are in part similar to the other archaic objects, but the men feeding long-necked mythical beasts recall the designs on the so-called castanets of the Middle Kingdom. Fig 4, see PL. VI.

6, 8. Hind and foreleg of bull, much conventionalised, treated in exactly the same style as similar pieces found at Naqada (*Tombeau Royal*) and Abydos. The raised lines representing veins (?) are almost identical in all the pieces found.

7. Fragment of a human foot wearing a sandal, with heel strap and broad side-piece; see sandals in the servant's hand on the great slate, PL. XXIX.

PL. XVII. 1. Limestone vase, nearly solid, with two scorpion signs in relief on the shoulder.

2. Vase of serpentine with lion-head handles, pierced horizontally, and the sign *set* in relief below.

3. Carved ivory handle (?) like those of PL. XIII. The wavy-necked animal may be intended for a giraffe, or for one of the mythical beasts of XVI. 2. At Beni Hasan their name is given as *ses.*

PL. XVIII. 1. Baboon of limestone, carrying its young.

2. Plaque of green glaze, shown both back and front, similar to the plaques from the doorway of Neterkhet, preserved in Berlin.

The plaque here photographed came from the main deposit, but another like it was found under the brickwork of a mastaba in the cemetery.

The Y-shaped mark above the oblong projection on the back was made before firing. The black number on the side is only a reference to our notebooks.

3. A small female figure of lapis lazuli; the head is missing, but the wooden peg by which it was attached rémains. The flat shape, the position of the hands, and the general style of the figure are very similar to those of the Greek island figures, made of alabaster and limestone. It was found a little to the south of the main deposit and underneath one of the brick walls.

4. Minute figure of a child, in chrysocolla, finely finished.

5. Hawk of limestone, found in the temple, but *not* in main deposit: it is doubtless of later date than the rest and has been put in this plate by error, as also has

6. A fragment of a diorite bowl with the name of Khufu incised; this too does not come from the main deposit.

7. Dwarf in green glaze; wears a necklace.

8. Small vase with horizontally-pierced handles: made of green glaze.

9. Green glaze; unrecognised animal.

10. Frog of alabaster.

11. Frog of rock-crystal.

12. Stand for a vase; limestone.

13. Model of a pot containing flour (?); green glaze.

14. Frog of serpentine.

15. Scorpion of serpentine, finely finished.

16. Tail of a large scorpion of rock crystal: the end is pierced with two holes for pegging on to the body.

17. Mace of rock crystal, oval in cross section.

18. Cow (?) in green glaze.

19. Dwarf of limestone.

20. Object of glazed quartz of unknown use. In shape it is like the handle of a vase, nearly cylindrical; the back is flat but has several grooves running at right angles to the axis of the cylinder. A hole is pierced near each end from the grooved side to the central tube.

21. Fragment from the edge of a great porphyry vase, in shape and size similar to that shown on PL. XXXVII. 4, but with fluted surface. The inscription must have run round the horizontal part of the rim. This vase had been broken into a large number of small fragments, some of which were found widely scattered over the temple site. The greater part was missing. The surface is mostly whitened, so as to show up the carving free of the colours of the stone.

22. Portion of a scorpion.

PL. XIX. 1. Limestone vase with design in relief: this is developed on the right side of the plate. Phot. on PL. XX. 1, and XXV.

2. Basket of fish in steatite. Phot. PL. XX. 7.

3. Limestone mace in form of double ram's head. Phot. in PL. XXV.

4. Part of a *hotep* sign made of gold foil. Phot. PL. XX. 9. The eyelet holes on the base show that it was sewn together, as was the handle of the archaic knife published by De Morgan (*Tombeau Royal,* PL. V.). [Probably peg holes for fastening to a wooden core.—F. P.]

5. Scorpion in malachite. Phot. PL. XX. 10.

6. Development of the design round a steatite macehead, the view of which is given on PL. XXIII. The animals are dogs wearing collars and name-plates (?), alternating with lions.

PL. XX. 1. Limestone vase, see last plate.

2. Duck-shaped pot of serpentine.

3. An object in green glaze, apparently a fruit.

4. Duck-shaped vase of steatite.

5, 6. Green glaze: these are possibly maceheads.

7. Lower and upper view of the basket of fish in steatite. The basket appears to be made of a large leaf (?).

8. Hippopotamus (?): limestone.

9. The *hotep* sign of gold foil.

10. Scorpion of malachite.

11. Vase on stand: green glaze.

12. Hyæna (?) : green glaze.

13. Ape (?) : glaze.

14. Green glaze.

PL. XXI. All green glaze.

1. Vase with discontinuous wavy handle.

2, 3. See Phot. PL. XXII. 3. Prisoner with arms tied behind his back, dressed in girdle with sheath (see Naville, *Recueil*, 1900) in front.

4. See Phot. XXII. 4. Scorpion : legs shown in but slight relief, claws omitted.

5. See Phot. XXII. 7. Calf with legs tied together.

6, 8. See Phot. XXII. 5, 9. Perhaps maceheads.

7. See Phot. XXII. 8. Wild boar ; this should be drawn with a long square snout ; the piece was lost and not found again till too late for the publication.

9. See Phot. PL. XXII. 6. Lid of a vase.

10. See Phot. XXII. 11. This is the rudest type of monkey, cut out of a flat slab of paste and with the edges hardly rounded.

11. See Phot. XXII. 12. Monkey holding a vase (?).

12–16. See PL. XXII. 10, 17, 14, 16, 18. A squat vase, a gazelle or ibex, a hawk, a pelican, and a fish.

PL. XXII. 1. A vase in green glaze.

2. Baboon in green glaze—a good specimen of the more finished type.

Most of the rest are drawn on the last plate.

PL. XXIII. Various green glazed beads ; the sceptre head, drawn in PL. XIX. 6. ; inscription of Khasekhemui, see PL. II. 3.

PL. XXIV. Nos. 1 to 10 are from the main deposit. The others are undated so far as evidence from this site goes.

1 and 3. Spiral beads of green glaze. Of these a large number, no less than 1400, were found in a heap. There are two kinds, one flat-ended, the other, shown at the top of each string, bevelled at one end.

2. Copper dagger. Two holes are drilled through the tang to attach the wooden handle, traces of which remain.

4. Chisel of glazed quartz. The thin green glaze (once blue), shows dark in the photograph : more of it remains than is usual on such objects : where the thin film of glaze has decayed and fallen away the bared surface of quartz has a high polish.

This technique was presumably an imitation of turquoise.

5. Unknown object of glazed quartz : the end on the right is pierced with two holes at right angles.

6, 7, 8. Tablets of glazed quartz of unknown use ;

7 and 8 are pierced with two L-shaped holes running from the end to one flat side. They may possibly have been used for inlay in wood or stone, like the plaques of green glazed pottery.

9. Claws of a scorpion, of serpentine.

10. Tail of a scorpion, of limestone.

11 to 27 are all flints.

11. Part of a knife.

15. Very smooth.

17. Early period of Naqada ; these flints are probably daggers, a fine specimen with gold handle having been lately acquired by the Cairo Museum. [Forked lance heads, see *Naqada*, pp. 50, 51 ; afterwards used ceremonially, see *Man*, 1902, No. 64.— F.P.].

19. Part of a bracelet.

21. An adze head (?) ; similar ones were found in great numbers at Naqada scattered over the desert, in and near the cemetery ; they have not been discovered in tombs.

22. A snake (?).

24 to 27. These three-limbed flints have been found in other sites, but never in dated positions.

PL. XXV. 1. All flint knives from the main deposit. The first is a much worn implement ; the second is of the regular Old Kingdom type, while the large central one is closely similar to those from the Mena tomb. Nos. 4 and 5 are more like the daggers from Naqada of earlier date. The curved instrument below (43 c.m. long) is perhaps a model of a throw-stick.

The great variety of types in this group certainly does not support our view that all the objects of the main deposit are of the same date.

2. The two great limestone maces shown in detail in PL. XXVI. B. and C. ; between them is the limestone vase of PL. XX., a large fluted mace of dolerite, and another of the sharp edged type, on the edge of which leans a third, smaller, of rock-crystal and oval in cross section. To the left are four more, a large one of quartz, another of alabaster with spiral grooves, the two-headed mace already shown, and, in the corner, a specimen of the ordinary limestone mace of which so many were found ; this one is however of a shorter and thicker shape than most.

It will be noticed that of the larger of the two decorated maces only about a half was found ; but that it is of a hard stone with better preserved surface, and with the decoration in higher relief than in the smaller one.

PL. XXVIA. Fragments of a great mace, not

from the main deposit, but found among a lot of limestone chips at a high level near the west end of the five chambers at the N. of the temple. The ground had been probably much disturbed, and no conclusion can be drawn from the position.

The first photograph shows the king seated in a shrine as in XXVIB.

The second and the fourth (below 2) show a human head with large pig-tail, above which is a curved rope. The figure to which the head belongs must have been sitting, for the lower line of the register can be seen not far below. Perhaps it was carried in a palanquin. The hand-like object above I do not understand.

The remaining fragment, from the lower part of the mace, has two registers; in the upper one are three figures walking; in the lower are two men (and part of a third) wearing caps with long tassels (or hair?). One carries a vase, another holds in his hand one of those tails which were worn at this period by ordinary men and later by the king alone. [This type with long plaited pigtail is also known at Abydos, and probably belonged to the Red Sea mountains. *Jour. Anthrop. Inst.* XXXI., PL. XIX.—F. P.].

5. Model of a couch or similar object, 67 c.m., or 26 inches, long; made of a mottled pink and white limestone: the pieces were found, separated and broken, at different points in the main deposit. The rows of small holes leading from the upper edges to the inner side, both of the long and the cross pieces, show that the space between them was covered by a net, perhaps of leather thongs. There are 29 holes in each of the long pieces, the end two being used for lacing on the cross bars. Twelve of these holes (diam. 7 m.m.) are larger than the rest (6 m.m.) and the line of them is 3 m.m. behind the latter. Their openings too on the inside are lower (by 4 m.m.). The cross pieces have each 15 holes, all in one line, and of the same size (7 m.m. inside, 8 outside). On the inner sides of the long bars is a ledge 5 m.m. wide; and on the upper edge, near the ends, are four holes larger than those for the thongs. These may have held uprights for a roof to the couch. The four holes half-way down the side of the long pieces, a pair near each end, would be used for thongs, or wooden rods, to stiffen the whole structure. At the best it would not seem very rigid, and can hardly have been carried about.

PL. XXVIB. The limestone mace to the right of the photograph on PL. XXV. is here shown in detail. The upper half of the plate contains 12 photographs, 6 of the upper part of the mace, and 6 of the lower: as, owing to the curvature of the surface it is impossible to show the whole of a vertical sector on one plate. Below is a drawing by Mr. Green, in which the whole design is developed. The accuracy of the drawing may thus be checked.

The mace is made of a rather soft limestone; at one point there is a bad break, most of the fine outer surface has disappeared, and some unsightly grooves have been eaten out by the roots of neighbouring plants. There is a hole for a handle, 4·5 c.m. at the ends, narrowing slightly at the middle. The height of the mace is 19·5 c.m. (7·6 ins.), its diameter 18·8 (7·4 ins.), and the relief of the design about 1 m.m.

The central figure, towards which the others face, is the king, his Horus name being behind him at the top of the scene. He is seated on a throne in a shrine reached by a stair of 9 steps; he wears the crown of Lower Egypt, and a long robe reaching to the feet, and holds in his hand a scourge.

Above the shrine hovers the protecting vulture, drawn in the same singular manner as on the ivory cylinder of XV. 7.

Below the king stand two fan-bearers; perhaps we should understand them as being really one on each side of the throne. Behind are two rows of figures, meant, of course, to be on the same level. Three of them are servants with staves; the other two are the scribe Thet and the servant with sandals and a metal ewer, who both appear again on the great slate palette.

Before the shrine are three registers. In the upper one are four standard-bearers, the same four as on the slate palette, but in a different order; in both the standard-bearer of Khonsu differs from the rest in being beardless.

In the middle register is a figure seated in a palanquin covered with basket-work. Who this may be it is difficult to say. In the reliefs from Abusir, which depict somewhat similar scenes, the figures in palanquins are the royal children (Borchardt, and compare PL. XXVIc. 2); but here the mention of great numbers of oxen, etc., and comparison with the slate palette, would suggest that a review of captives and booty is depicted. So the figure may be a captive king, as Prof. Petrie suggests, or the Tikanou or human sacrifice as it has been explained by M. Maspéro.

Behind the palanquin are three bearded figures. The middle one wears the small kilt or tassel which, in several of these monuments is the dress of enemies.

(As XXIX., XXII. 3, but in II. 1 worn by an Egyptian, unless we take the statue to be prae-Egyptian.)

Their hands are clasped on their breasts in an attitude of respect, or perhaps tied, and they seem to be dancing. Their knees are more bent than those of the Egyptians, and though their attitude is not that of the dancers in the last plate, the crescent-shaped signs on each side of them must be the same as those on the tablet of Den (PETRIE *R. T.* XI. 14), the scene of Usertesen before Min (*Koptos* IX.), and other instances, in all of which a king is shown dancing before a god. (For the sign see GRIFFITH, *Hieroglyphs*, p. 64.) The figures may then be captives dancing in worship of the king. The enclosure with oxen, above the palanquin, can be taken for part of the booty.

The third register shows an ox, a goat, and a human captive followed by high numbers. "Oxen 400,000, goats 1,422,000, captives 120,000."

To the right of the scene an ibis, an upright sign, looped or split at the top, and a vase on a stand, have no obvious connection with the rest.

Below is a park containing large antelopes. The wavy line may be an attempt to represent a moat of water round the enclosure.

[This mace head is of Narmer, who was apparently the next king but one before Mena, see *Royal Tombs* ii. 5; for a more complete description of some scenes see *Hierakonpolis* i. 9. The ibis is on a shrine, with an offering-vase before it, see the shrine in *Royal Tombs* ii., PL. X. 2.—F. P.]

PL. XXVIc. The larger and incomplete mace of PL. XXV.

1, 5, 7, show the top register, a row of nome standards, from each of which is hung a *rekhyt* bird by its neck. The standards are the jackal (fig. 7), Set, Min (with feather above), another Set, and the hill sign. On the other side of the mace was another series of standards (fig. 5), from each of which hung a bow. The *rekhyt* and the bows were, doubtless, both symbolical of definite races—the *rekhyt* of some subject race in Egypt itself, the bow of foreigners.

The lower part of the mace is occupied by a scene of irrigation, of opening of a canal, or the like, and has been interpreted by Maspero as the ceremony of *Khebs-ta* (*Rev. Crit.*, Mai., 1901).

The king holds a hoe; a servant before him carries a basket; these are, as is well known, the tools which, to the present day, take the place of the spade in northern countries.

The name of the king, or his title and name, a seven-petaled flower with a scorpion, is before him, and two standard-bearers are seen further to the right. The king stands by the side of a canal in which three men are working; one of them carries a hoe in his hand. On the edge of the stone is seen the prow of a ship; next to it is a palm-tree enclosed in a *seriba*, and at the bottom of all is a house with upright pillars and roofed with mat-work (?). There is a similar house on a fragment of a slate palette in the British Museum (see P. S. B. A., vol. xxii.).

PL. XXVII. shows the great variety of shapes in the mace-heads of the main deposit. The partially perforated shapes, like 25 and 27, show that none of these objects were weapons; they can only have been of ceremonial use.

The flat, sharp-edged mace was rare as compared with the pear-shaped type.

PL. XXVIII. shows the two sides of the smaller decorated slate palette.

The scenes are flanked by two jackals whose heads were carved in the round. Only one head was recovered; the signs of mending below the other show that it had been broken in antiquity and repaired, and probably broken again.

On the *front*, in the middle, is the saucer-shaped depression for paint. The rest of the field is occupied by desert scenes. Two monsters, with lions' heads and bodies, and enormous snake-like necks, are licking the body of a gazelle (?) before devouring it, while three jackals and a vulture wander round the prey.

Below this, four antelopes of different kinds—gazelle (?), ibex, oryx and hartebeest (?)—are hunted by three lop-eared hounds, which wear collars.

On the *back* is another picture of the beasts which existed, or were believed to exist, in the desert. At the top, two gazelles are attacked by a pair of lions. One of the snake-necked monsters seizes an oryx by the leg. A leopard has just overtaken a wild sheep. Then come a jackal, an antelope with lyre-shaped horns (? hartebeest), and an *akhekh*, most swift of beasts, with wings and a hawk's head; and below are a wild ox (?), an ibex, a giraffe, and a jackal (?); the last wears a girdle and plays upon a pipe.

The identifications of several of the animals have been suggested by Captain Flower.

PL. XXIX. The great slate palette of Narmer.

The side shown on the left it is better to call the front of the palette, as the circular depression on this side must be the essential part, that in which green paint was mixed. Similar palettes were used by all

G

the archaic people to grind the paint with which they adorned their faces. This can now hardly be doubted. Many hundreds of slate palettes have been found in the different cemeteries; they are placed in front of the face, and the objects found near them are toilet articles, such as beads, combs, and hairpins. Very often they have a depression worn in the middle, sometimes on both sides; this depression is generally stained green with powdered malachite, and the pebble for grinding lies near it. Little leathern bags containing malachite chips, and shells containing the powdered mineral mixed with fat, were found in several cases close to the palette.. Finally, on two steles of the Old Kingdom at Cairo, traces of green paint on the cheek-bones, and not on the lower part of the face, are plainly to be seen. (The peculiar pendants of the Uza eye would be well explained as representing streaks of this paint.) The argument, then, is singularly strong that the simpler palettes were used for face-paint.

And this decorated palette belongs to the same class. The shape—a derivative, probably, of the double bird-head type—is known, and the gap betweeen this piece and the plain slabs of slate of the private tombs of Naqada is not entirely unbridged. Incised drawings of animals are not very uncommon on the poorer palettes, and one was sold in Cairo lately decorated with three ostriches and a human figure in relief. We may suppose that this sumptuous palette was given to the temple by Narmer, to be used in dressing either the local idol or the king himself before some religious ceremony.

The front of the palette is divided into four registers. In the first is the name of the king flanked by two Hathor heads. It is strange to find the *ka* name written without the hawk above; not less so that in so early a monument the door patterns should be so simplified and different on the two sides of the palette. The name is written with two signs, that of the large fish with tentacles (*Heterobranchus anguillaris ?*), which in the tomb of Thy is called *Ndr*, and the chisel with blade on one side, reading *mer*. The king has, therefore, been generally called Nar-mer, though it is by no means certain that this is the correct reading.

In the second register the king is seen marching to the right; his name, this time without the frame, is repeated before him. He is preceded by the official Thet, and followed by a servant bearing his sandals and a metal ewer. The word Thet may be a name, or may be the word for scribe. There is much detail in the dress of the three figures; the shirt-like garment of the king fastened over the left shoulder, the two flaps of beadwork over his skirt, one square-ended, the other pointed, and with a bird ornament at the end; the dress of Thet, with its two pendants over the left shoulder; and the curious triangular object (basket?) worn by the servant at his waist.

The square label over the servant's head, bearing the sign *deb* (?), must be either the title of the whole scene, or the name of the place from which the king has come. Capart has read it "Edfu."

The name or title of the servant is written with a rosette, 6 leaved in this case, 7 leaved on the other side, and with the sign *hen*. Petrie would translate this "royal servant," but it may be equally well a name.

Before the king go four standard-bearers carrying the symbols of four deities; one is the object which has been called a piece of meat, and also a lock of hair; the next is a jackal, and the remaining pair are hawks. These recur in similar scenes at Bubastis and Deir el Bahri, but with the substitution of the ibis for one of the hawks.

Note that the standard-bearer nearest Thet has no beard, wears a round wig, and a short skirt; the next is bearded, has a square-bottomed headdress, and shows over his shoulder one of the same pendants of which Thet shows two. The remaining two standard-bearers wear tassels or kilts in front, and are dressed alike. It is possible that this difference of dress on official occasions may show a survival from the times when the different towns of Egypt had their own customs and dress, as well as their own gods.

The king has come to view the ten bodies on the right of the scene. They lie with arms tied together; their heads, all but one covered with a double-horned headdress, are removed, and placed between their legs. Above the bodies are four signs. The first two may be read "the great gate," and the other two, the bird on a harpoon with a boat below, have some connection with a festival.

This scene is discussed by Naville (*Recueil*, vol. xxi.), who suggests that it represents the "festival of the destruction of the Anu," an important festival in the early times, as the Palermo stone shows. The mention on the other side of the palette of a definite number of prisoners, would lead us to suppose that it commemorates a victory by Narmer himself.

In the second register is the circular depression which was the essential part of the palette; it is bounded by the necks of two monstrous animals, with leopards' heads and bodies. The spaces above them are filled by two men, with a very peculiar dress, which does not occur again on this series of monuments. Note that they wear a short skirt in addition to, and apparently under, the peculiar sheath or apron in front (cf. NAVILLE, *Figurines; Recueil*, vol. xxii.). An extraordinary parallel to this scene from Chaldea has been pointed out by Heuzey (*Compt. Rendu. Acad. Inscr. et B. L.*, 1899, p. 66).

In the fourth register we have a scene of regular Egyptian type. The king, represented as a bull, breaks down the wall of a city, and tramples the inhabitants under foot. The sign within the fortress is presumably its name.

On the other side of the palette the king smites with his club the head of a kneeling foe; behind him is his servant with the sandals; before him is the hawk-god of Hierakonpolis with one bird's foot, and one human arm holding a cord, which passes through the lip of the human-headed block below it. From this block rise seven papyrus stems. Erman has pointed out that these are "thousand" signs united at the base; a similar sign is to be seen on the smaller of the two decorated maces, and occurs even in the pyramid texts (*Mirinri*, l. 403, p. 255). But the undoubted "thousands" flowers on the mace are not quite the same as those in question here, and it is more probable that the plant of the north is intended, and that the scene represents a victory over the Semitic tribes of the north. The type of face of the enemy is very different from that of the king, and agrees with the later Egyptian portrayals of Semites.

The Hathor-head ornaments on the king's kilt should be noted; there is, perhaps, some meaning in the fact that these are worn with the white crown, but the bird ornament with the red.

In the lowest register are seen two of the enemy dead and stripped; above their heads are the names of their towns or nations. The length of the palette is 63 c.m. (25 inches), its thickness varying from 15 m.m. at some parts of the edge to 4 c.m. in the middle; the front face is slightly convex, but wavy and irregular; the back is much flatter. The surface is smooth, but not polished, everywhere showing scratches and tool-marks. This monument is quite perfect, not having suffered from the salt and moisture which had destroyed so many of the other objects.

PL. XXX. 1–5. Stone vases of coarse work from the main deposit.

6, 7. Alabaster bowls with hieroglyphs, drawn on PL. XXXIV.

PL. XXXI. 1. Boat-shaped dish of serpentine with two serpents below.

2. This shape occurs in obsidian in the Menes tomb.

3. Compound vase: it must have had a lid in two pieces.

6. Similar shapes both in pottery and stone are known from archaic burials.

PL. XXXII. 1. The baboon is roughly formed, owing to the hardness of the chert.

2. The pieces of green glazed tile show the cast of the palm-leaf mat on which it was made upon the inner side, and the ribbed face on the outer side.

5, 6. The pieces of ivory wand are drawn on PL. XVI.

PL. XXXIII. 1. Limestone, solid; drawn on PL. XVII.

The tall vase (alabaster) is interesting as showing the wavy pattern, still discontinuous, but not used as a handle.

PL. XXXIV. The series of shapes of roughly-made alabaster dishes, of which a large number were found; many had rudely scratched inscriptions of two signs each. There are traces of blue frit in the signs. Of these inscriptions there are three; in all occurs the *Ka* sign with arms hanging, and the other three signs are: (1) the hawk on a crescent or boat, (2) the scorpion, and (3) the hawk perched on one hand of a *Ka* sign.

PL. XXXV. Shapes of pottery from the main deposit. Most of the pots were of very coarse ware, the "black and red" being only found in degraded forms (12, 13).

PL. XXXVI. Drawings of the three great stone vases. Those of diorite and alabaster are shown again on the next plate. The granite vase was found on the E. edge of the main deposit; it is very heavy, as may be seen by the section; the surface is smooth, but not finely polished, and the handles are mere cylindrical lugs.

PL. XXXVII. 1. A large alabaster vase, 80 c.m. high; found on the revetment, at a point to the N. of the main deposit, where the archaic walls butt on the revetment. The vase stood upright; its mouth was closed by a flat earthenware dish; its base was about 1 m. above the foot of the revetment; it had then been intentionally buried at a time when the revetment was already largely hidden under the soil.

2. Inscription on the alabaster, photographed on larger scale. See PL. XXXVIII.

3. A fragment, the only one found, of an alabaster bowl (diameter roughly ·2 m). The inscription is the same as the one above.

4. Great vase of diorite (?), from a point close to the main deposit on the north. The mouth was closed by a flat pottery dish. The work of this is extremely fine, but it has no inscription. Height, 344 m.m. (13½ ins.), diameter, 584 m.m (23 ins.), thickness of sides, 3 c.m. Now at Manchester.

PL. XXXVIII. 1, 2. Copies of the inscriptions on two of the three great vases. That from the granite vase was drawn from a squeeze, and the form of this flower sign in the word Nekheb is not quite certain, as some crystals are broken out there. Further, there are traces of another *sekhem* sign, never finished, in the name of the king. The two inscriptions are the same. The king's *ka* name, Khasekhem, is faced by the vulture goddess of El Kab holding a *Sam* sign in one foot, and in the other a circlet enclosing the word *besh* (rebel ?).

Above are the words "in Nekheb" and the four signs on the right with the palm rod flanking them probably mean "the festival," or "the year of fighting the northern people."

The form of the flower sign in "Nekheb" is not accidental ; see XXXVII. 3.

PL. XXXIX. The middle part of this statue of Khasekhem was not found ; the head and the lower part lay together in the middle of the main deposit, while the similar statue of green slate (PL. XLI.) was found with the copper statue of Pepy.

The first three photographs show the face under different lights, the middle two give the whole head, while below are two views of the lower part. The base has been rubbed with chalk to show up the design lightly scratched upon it, see PL. XL.

The presence of paint-lines on the face forms an exception to Borchardt's canon that these lines do not appear before the VIth Dynasty.

PL. XL. The inscriptions round the bases of the two statues of Khasekhem of PLS. XXXIX. and XLI. They are clearly meant to be identical. On the back and sides are rude figures of the dead, lying in fantastic attitudes. The style of drawing is curiously unlike that of most Egyptian art, in which a firm unbroken line, drawn in with one sweep, defines a great part of a figure. Here the line is drawn bit by bit, retouched, and, as it were, painted in. [A style due to scratching on a hard stone.—F. P.]

On the front of the base is the word *seb*, determined by the prostrate bound figure, with the sign of the north on his head, and followed by the number 47209.

The Horus name of the king is very lightly incised on the top of the base, just before the feet. On the limestone statue the name is fairly clear, Kha sekhem ; on the other the name was at first read *Heq*, but the stroke joining the horizontal and vertical signs is very faint and probably accidental. It is, however, surprising to find such carelessly made signs on so early a monument.

PL. XLI. 1. The slate statue of Khasekhem, found with the copper group of Pepy and his son, and with the pottery lion of PL. XLV.

Only half of the head was secured though a wide and careful search was made, and it is probable that the statue was broken and incomplete when buried.

The king wears the crown of Upper Egypt ; he is dressed in a long robe, like that used in the Sed festivals. The left hand is across the body, the right stretched on the knee. In the clenched fist is a hole, 8 m.m. in diameter, for a mace or whip. He has no beard, and no paint-lines to the eyes.

The throne is a simple one, with a short back, a sunk panel on each side, and two panels one above the other at the back. There is considerable finish in the detail of hands and feet, but no attempt to undercut these parts, nor is the space between the feet cut out flat ; there is, too, a certain roundness of style in the whole figure. These points are mentioned, because at first sight there is a resemblance to late work ; and, had it not been for the scratchings on the base, the statue would have been attributed by many to the Saite period.

2. PLS. XLII., XLIII. Photograph of the golden head of the hawk of copper plate, found in the central chamber of the group at the north of the temple. Details are in the next two plates, and a diagram of the hawk on its stand in PL. XLVII.

The photograph shows the head as originally mounted at the Cairo Museum, and is incorrect in three particulars : the double plume should be turned right round (through 180°) and sunk so that the two sheaths fall just inside the circlet ; and a gold nail should be seen projecting from the lower of the two holes in the central line of the plumes. The circlet is correctly raised above the bird's head.

Plumes, circlet and head are of beaten gold, the

head being made from a single mass; the plate varies in thickness from ½ m.m. near the edge to 2 m.m. near the beak. The eyes are formed by the brightly-polished ends of an obsidian rod, which passes right through the head. A copper rod found fitting inside the circlet, had been used for attaching the plume. In the base can be seen a series of nails, some of gold, others, much rusted, of copper. Of these nails seven behind and three in front were of gold, while five nails on the right side and seven on the left were of copper. Some of the red rust of old gold still remains, especially inside the head where it has been less handled. The outer surface is smooth and polished, but the inside is covered with round punch marks. The incised lines marking the nostrils, and the lines round the eyes, were made with a punch or chisel, and there are corresponding raised lines inside.

The eyelids are in sharp relief, but appear to be beaten up from the plate, and not to be separate pieces soldered on. On the top of the head is a square hole, 24 m.m. in the side, cut with a chisel from inside.

The curve of the base curiously does not fit what remains of the bird's body. The copper nails are so much corroded that their shape cannot be seen; those of gold are thick and square, with small heads and short points. Two or three similar nails were found at the lowest level, in a different part of the temple, rather to the south of the revetment. Were these dropped from the idol before the revetment was covered with earth, or built over by the walls of the temple?

The marks round the eye are unlike those ordinarily found on figures of hawks. Here the pendant below the eye is pointed and sloping: the curved mark behind the eye has a re-entrant angle inside, and a sharp point on the outer side; and the lines above the eye are plain. The usual shape is as follows: the forward pendant is vertical, round at the base and connected with the curved line behind: this latter is sickle-shaped and is serrated above. This is the case in the gold hawk-headed clasp of a necklace from the tomb of Fu-ab-ra (De Morgan, *Dahchour*, fig. 230), in a similar clasp inlaid with lapis lazuli found in the Dahshur treasure, in another (No. 962) from Aahhotep, in a fine bronze hawk inlaid with gold, and in another hawk of limestone with a bronze base. (The two last are in the Pantheon Room, Cairo.)

The circlet is a strip of gold, 21 to 24 m.m. in breadth and ½ m.m. thick, bent round so as to overlap

15 m.m.; the ends are fastened together, and to the asp by three gold rivets. The edges of the strip are rather sharp. The asp is of thicker plate, with rounded edges. The ornament is incised.

In the plumes a gold nail (round, thin, 3 c.m. long) was found projecting from the lower of the two holes in the middle, point forward; there must then have been in front of the plume a part of the head-dress made of wood, or some such material.

Two sheaths, made of strips of gold plate, are soldered to projections below. The burr of the nail-holes is on the same side as these sheaths, which were therefore in front. The sheaths were, no doubt, attached to the copper rod, which was found inside the circlet. On the back of the plumes there remain some of the lines which were scratched with a graver to mark the pieces which were to be cut out.

The main dimensions are as follows:—

Total height of head and plumes, about 36 c.m.,				14·1 ins.
Height of head	.	.	. 10 c.m.,	3·9 ins.
Diameter of circlet .	.	.	. 7·5 to 8 c.m.,	3·0 ins.
Height of plume	.	.	. 252 m.m.,	9·9 ins.
Weight of plume	.	.	. 196 grams,	6¾ ozs.
„ „ circlet	.	.	. 75 grams,	2⅝ ozs.
„ „ head (without obsidian)	.	325 grams,	10½ ozs.
Total weight of gold	.	.	. 596 grams,	19¾ ozs.

PL. XLIV. Photograph on PL. XLV. A lion of coarse pottery, black in the interior, red outside, painted with haematite and finely polished. Statues in this very distinctive material have been found at Koptos, the Ramesseum, Medinet Habu and Abydos.

This lion was buried with the copper statue of Pepy and the green slate statue of Khasekhem; fragments of another were found at the lowest level in another part of the temple site. The nearest parallel in style is afforded by the lions on the alabaster table of offerings in the first room at Cairo, attributed to the third dynasty (No. 1322 in new catalogue). The position of the broken statue also shows that this one must be of very early date.

2. A sheet of copper with embossed inscription, mentioning the Sed festival and giving the titles of Pepy I. It was found as a crumpled mass adhering to the breast of the copper statue (*v.* PL. XLV.)

PL. XLVI. These inscriptions are all later than the objects before described; 7 and 11 are interesting as showing the appearance of the idol of the Hiera-konpolis temple in later times.

PL. XLVII. has been already described with the objects in PLS. XLI.–XLV.

PL. XLIX. The scale of this plate is wrongly

marked. Nos. 22 to 27 are large vases, scale probably ₁₀.

PLS. L.–LVI. show the copper statues of Pepy and his son. The inscription from the base is drawn on PL. XLIV. and photographed on PL. XLV. The position in which the group was found is indicated in the sketch on PL. XLVII. The small statue, separated into three pieces, lay inside the body of the greater one. The legs of this were laid over the trunk. The lion of red pottery (PL. XLV.) and the green stone statue of Khasekhem (PL. XLI.) lay touching the copper group. The thin metal plate with the titles of Pepy had been crumpled up and placed on the chest of the statue to which the green rust had caused it to adhere. Chemical change had made this sheet of metal, like the statues themselves, very brittle, and we broke it in removal; but when first torn from the base it had clearly been quite flexible.

The relation of this to the statues, and the fact that the two figures had formed a group was pointed out by Borchardt at the Cairo Museum, when Barsanti made his very careful restoration. This was a long task. The small figure adhered to the larger at several points, and it was hard to extract it without doing damage. One error in the mounting will be noticed, an error which can, happily, be easily remedied. The body of the smaller statue should be raised somewhat; the thighs are now (PL. LIV.) too short. The hips, as those of Pepy, must have been made of some other material.

The metal of the statues is copper, the whole being beaten out of plates, which overlapped and were fastened together, and to a core, presumably of wood, by closely-set rows of copper nails. It is very surprising to find the oldest metal statues made by so difficult a process, a process, too, not hitherto known in Egypt; but there can be no doubt on the point. The joints of the metal can clearly be seen, even from the outside; and on the inside, the long rows of nails still exist, running down the inside of the arms, the sides of the body and the back of the legs. The nails are pointed, and the ends have never been turned; they are certainly not rivets, and unless there had been a core of wood or some such material, it would have been almost impossible to fix them.

The fact that the hips are missing, while the base of the trunk and the tops of the thighs have unbroken edges, shows, too, that this part of the body was made of some other material than copper. The back of Pepy's head, too, is missing, though the metal edges of the part remaining are even and rounded, and show no sign of ancient fracture.

We must assume then that the statue was beaten to fit over a core of wood, to which the plates were then nailed. The hips were doubtless covered with a kilt; some fine plaster with a fluted surface remains on one thigh, and this was probably gilt. The hands are of thicker metal than most of the body, and must have offered special difficulties to the work of the hammer. The thought occurred to several of us that they might have been made separately of cast metal, but of this there is no evidence.

The construction of the head of the Pepy can be seen from behind. The pupil, a disc of black stone, probably obsidian, is set in an eyeball of white limestone, and this is retained in its place by an ouch of copper projecting inside the head. A plug of plaster fills up the tubular hole in the eyeball, and prevents the pupil from falling backwards (see diagram, PL. XLVII).

There are nails on the top edge of the forehead, seven in front, one near the ear, and four near the right jaw. There is a joint down the left side of the neck, and here, too, there is a triangular patch, where the metal gave out and the plates failed to meet. The sides of the patch are about 10, 8, and 8 c.m.; there are twelve nails in the top side of the triangle, which is horizontal, one and six in the other two respectively.

Inside the trunk there are long rows of nails running down the two sides. The arms are made of separate plates joining on the shoulder, with the arm-pieces overlapping (observed on left side only). The nails attaching them are very close together, there being forty-two to one arm, all of them on the top and sides of the joint, for the armpit was not accessible to the hammer.

On the top of the shoulders the chest and back plates are joined by another row of nails; on the left shoulder, perhaps also on the right, there are two rows, 1 c.m. apart.

The front plate naturally overlaps the back. The arms are made with the joint running down the inside. The left forearm is attached to the upper arm just below the elbow. No nails were seen in the fist.

The lower edge of the trunk is smooth and flat, except on the two sides where the line is broken by the cutting out of two curved pieces. That on the left is semicircular, 5 c.m. in diameter; the opposite one is a smaller arc of a circle, 10 c.m. in the chord. These were evidently to adapt the metal to some projections in the wooden core, the nature of which is not clear.

In the right leg the seam goes down the back of the thigh, a little inside the median line, and continues down the calf. There are five nails round the top of the thigh, a group of three on the right side of the leg above the kneecap, and three more just below it. There are two small holes in the front of the thigh. Down the calf is a single row of nails, 1 c.m. apart. There is an extra nail in the middle of the calf, 2 c.m. to the left of the line of nails. The left half of the plate overlaps the right.

There is no base to the foot; the plate runs on slightly below the sole, and this lowest part is studded with nails 3 c.m. apart. The metal is pierced between the toes; the divisions were beaten through from above. The toes, on the other hand, seem to have been beaten out from the inside. There are traces of gilding on the toenails.

In the smaller statue the construction of the head cannot be so well seen, but in the photograph it will be noticed that the head-piece overlaps that of which the face is made, and that the line of junction is that of the hair. The ears were not found; they were evidently made separately and attached. On the forehead is a hole for the attachment of a uraeus.

The jointing on the shoulder, and the nails in the base of the trunk and the top of the thigh, can also be seen in the photograph.

As in the larger statue the joints run down each side of the trunk and down the back of the legs. In the right leg there is a double row of nails, one larger than the other. The larger, which project 5 to 7 m.m., run about 1 c.m. to the left of the smaller, which are but 2–4 m.m. long.

Some measures are added :—

Thickness of metal of the inscribed plate, 1 m.m.

Pepy statue.

Thickness of the metal in millimetres: of the foot, 4; thigh, 2; right arm, 4–5; neck, 2; chest at one point only, 1; left arm, 4; hand, 4 to 5.

	Metres.	Inches.
Height of trunk from tip of forehead to base	·78	30·7
Chest, greatest	1·03	40·5
Waist, least	·705	27·8
Between centres of pupils	·069	2·7
Round upper arm, left	·350	13·8
,, ,, right	·365	14·4
Forearm, left	·315	12·4
,, right	·310	12·2
Wrist, left	·225	8·9
,, right	·230	9·1
Height, left leg	·84	33·0
,, right ,,	·82	32·2

	Metres.	Inches.
Left leg from tip of second toe to top	·935	36·7
Length, left foot	·315	12·4
,, right ,,	·305	12·0
Girth, left thigh	·61	24·0
,, right ,,	·60	23·6
Below projection on thigh, left	·60	23·6
,, ,, right	·565	22·2
Girth of knee, left	·425	16·7
,, ,, right	·415	16·3
Above ankle, left	·295	11·6
,, ,, right	·285	11·2
Girth of calf of leg, left	·440	17·3
,, ,, right	·425 to ·430	16·8
Height of figure as now standing, only approximately correct	1·77	69·5

Smaller statue.

Thickness of metal in thigh, 2 m.m.; in hand, 3 m.m.

	Metres.	Inches.
Round upper arm, left	·14 (oxidised)	5·5
,, ,, right	·135	5·3
Round forearm, left	·127	5·0
,, ,, right	·127	5·0
Round wrist, left	·090	3·5
,, ,, right	·095	3·7
Round thigh, left	·210	8·3
,, ,, right (not measured).		
Round knee, left	·153	6·0
,, ,, right	·155	6·1
Round calf, left	·183	7·2
,, ,, right	·178	7·0
Above ankle, left	·123	4·8
,, ,, right	·118	4·6
Length of leg from top of thigh to tip of second toe, left	·337	13·3
Same, right	·288	11·3

The most striking point is the difference in the size of the legs; this arises from the convention of Egyptian art, which required the body to be erect, one leg to be advanced, and yet the foot to be planted flat on the floor. This could only be arranged by lengthening the advanced leg.

[The foregoing descriptions are all by J. E. Quibell, and the following by F. W. Green, down to PL. LXXII.]

PL. LVII. Archaic limestone statue from the northern gateway of the town wall. Ashmolean Museum, Oxford.

PL. LVIII. Fragments of two steles of the archaic period. The larger fragment was found in one of the storerooms in the S.E. side of the temple. The material is a dense quartzose rock of a dark slate-green colour, similar to that of some of the royal steles of the archaic period, found at Abydos. The design consists of two parts. On the upper is seen a figure, probably King Kha-sekhem, kneeling on a prostrate foe who is depicted with an aquiline nose, a beard, and flowing hair, similar to the captives on the palette of Narmer. On his head is a bow of the same shape as that in the hand of a soldier on a private stele from Abydos, now at Cairo.

From the position of the king's hand, it looks as if the sculptor had intended to show a cord attached to the prisoner's lip and held by the king. The body is shown of the same flattened shape to represent the hieroglyph of land as on the palette of Narmer.

In front of the figure of the king is the lower part of an inscription, which seems to read *t . ta . ;* the scene is bounded by a vertical line.

In the lower register is the *ka* name *Kha-sekhem*, surmounted by the hawk, above which is the conventional representation of the vault of heaven. To the left is a group of hieroglyphics which seem to be *debt-r-du-t,* or *debt-r-sem-t* ["humbling the foreign lands."—F. P.].

The whole design has been executed on a flat surface; the lines being made by hammering, and then smoothing down the groove produced by abrasion. The lower register, which is rather more finished, has an appearance of relief given to it by scraping away the outer edges of the grooves. This fragment is now in the Cairo Museum.

[The kneeling figure is evidently a captive, like that on Narmer's palette, held by the king, whose figure is entirely lost.—F. P.]

The lower fragment was not found with the first, but in earth that had already been disturbed. It may have formed part of the larger stone, but that is not probable. The scene represented is a row of kneeling figures or captives; the work is rough, and rather more deeply cut than the first. A number of fragments of the same rock, with one of the faces worked to a flat surface, were found on the site, generally at high levels. None were inscribed except those shown on PL. LVIII.

PL. LIX. 1. Part of the base of a limestone statuette of the archaic period, similar to those of King Kha-sekhem. The name may be that of King Zet, of the 1st Dynasty. The elaborate manner in which the panelling of the door is represented seems characteristic of this king. The fragment was found near to the broken stele of Kha-sekhem. Now in Ashmolean Museum, Oxford.

2. Alabaster vase from the archaic stratum, near the circular structures on the S.E. side of the temple.

3. Alabaster handle of a jar, in the form of a dog's or lion's head. The eyes have been fixed into the sockets by means of cement, traces of which

remain; the work seems archaic. Found in the Roman or Coptic houses on the S.W. side of the temple.

4, 5, 6, 7. Fragments of a large porphyry jar, which had been broken up and widely scattered. The rim shows a bird in relief, and part of a star-shaped object. The fragment 5 was found by Mr. Quibell; it has been reproduced here for comparison with the other fragments. The white paint was put on that the design might be more easily discerned. Oxford.

8. Cast of the inscription on a porphyry vase. The work is roughly scratched; over the panelling is seen the name Kha-sekhemui. Above it are the legs of the hawk. To the right is what appears to be the prow of a boat, but may be a badly represented *uas* sceptre. Found between the two enclosure walls on S.E. side of the temple, below the foot of the walls. Oxford.

9. Handle of serpentine dish or bowl, in the shape of a bull's head. Archaic period. Oxford.

PL. LX. 1. Curved flint knife of rather coarse work; from temple.

2. Curved knife of translucent flint. About 3 m.m. thick; of good workmanship; the under side is rather more carefully chipped than that shown.

3. Curved flint knife; more curved and thicker through than 1 and 2. From temple.

4. Curved flint knife, with the end worked to a point: under side is flatter than upper. Temple.

5. Long flint implement with worked point. From temple. All the above are scale 1 : 2.

6, 7, 8, 9, 10, 11, 12. Flint scrapers from the temple: 6 has a carefully-worked saw edge.

17. Flint hoe from house No. 172.

18. Fragment of flint hoe from temple site.

14. Tribrach flint, one of the points broken. The surface between the two upper points on both sides has been polished by use. The implement may be some kind of scraper.

PL. LX. 13. Flint axe, from a burial, in a large open-mouth jar or cist, found together with two or three small rough bottle-shaped vessels. From prehistoric cemetery.

19. Green jasper pounding or rubbing stone, from house No. 211.

PL. LXI. 1 and 2. Flint knife from the charcoal-discoloured stratum on the outside of the temple enclosure, near to the N.E. entrance.

3 and 6. Long flake of triangular section, one cutting edge finely worked. From grave 581, prehistoric cemetery. Ethnol. Mus., Camb.

4 and 5. Long flint flake of triangular section, one edge worked with extremely fine serrations, the fracture is ancient. From grave 542, prehistoric cemetery. Ethnol. Mus. Camb.

These implements are each shown in two different lights, so that the quality of the work may be better seen.

7 and 8. Fragment of one of the great flint knives from the main deposit. This fragment was found in the second season's work. It has been photographed on both sides. 7 shows the sun-pitted surface. The "skin" has been left on both faces.

Since the fragment was photographed, another piece of the same knife has been identified. The complete knife was about 64 c.m. long, 20 c.m. wide, and 6 c.m. thick, or 25 × 8 × 2½ ins. These flints were probably broken at the same time as the other archaic objects. Owing to the great size and poor cutting edge of these great flint implements it seems likely that they were used for purely ceremonial purposes. Baron von Hugel suggests as a parallel the ceremonial adzes from the eastern Pacific, a good example of which is preserved in the Cambridge Ethnological Museum.

9. Large flint implement from grave 166; prehistoric cemetery.

PL. LXII. 1. Ape's head in terra cotta. This head was found in the temple site, near to where the main deposit lay. It probably belongs to the same period. The material is a coarse red earthenware, which has suffered from the damp soil in which it was buried. There is a wooden peg for fastening the head on to the trunk.

This ape may have been a more elaborate example of the numerous small squatting apes made of green glaze, that were found with the main deposit. Oxford.

2. Donkey's head in terra-cotta, found near to the head of the ape, and probably also archaic; but as the earth in which it was buried had been disturbed it may be later. Oxford.

3. Diorite vase borer, showing the working surface. Compare XXXII. 3. Ethnol. Mus. Camb.

4. Block of quartz crystal, roughly chipped to shape, ready to be made into a bowl by grinding and boring. The borer shown on the top was not found in this position, but it is shown thus as it is about the size that would be used for the purpose. From House No. 144. Ethnol. Mus. Camb.

5. Group of three vase borers. The largest is of a rock similar to Gebel Ahmar sandstone. The two

smaller ones are of a similar gritty rock. The medium-sized borer was probably used to begin the boring operation, which was done by making a succession of holes of increasing diameter. This is well shown by part of a diorite bowl (now at the Cambridge Ethnological Museum) which has been bored by borers of two sizes; the smaller hole is almost exactly fitted by this grinder, while the larger has been executed by one about the same size as the largest of this group. The outside of the bowl has been finished first.

How the outside of the vases was ground and polished is not clear. No concave grinders such as would be required to work the outer surface were found. Perhaps a hollow was made in hard mud and lined with quick-cutting pieces of rock, the vase being rotated in this bed. In many cases the outside was finished by hand by a process analogous to filing, but in others it was ground and polished.

The manner in which these borers were used is shown on the reliefs. An upright rod forked at the lower end to take the borer is held in the left hand of the workman, who turns it with his right by means of a crank-like piece at the top. The whole is weighted down by heavy bags tied on with cords. A very good representation of this apparatus is shown on one of the false doors from Saqqarah, where the hieroglyphic *uba* is shown in great detail.

6. Group of three vase borers, probably for working softer rock than the others. The long-shaped example is of white limestone. Of the two others, the upper is of white quartzite and the lower of a cherty limestone. Ethnol. Mus. Camb.

PL. LXIII. 1. Limestone spindle whorl, marked with grooves to resemble a fossil echinoderm. Inscribed *wr* (?) From house in the Town, No. 211.

2. Baked clay seal. The impression on the broken part shows it to have been round a lump of papyrus. Inscribed on both sides and round the edge *Ha Neter-Khet Khenu*, see PL. LXX., No. 3. From house No. 186.

3. Part of a boat in dark, partly baked, clay, from archaic stratum of temple.

4. Limestone hemispherical spindle whorl, inscribed with a mark. From charcoal-discoloured stratum outside the N.E. entrance to the temple.

5. Dark baked clay cylinder, perforated like a cylinder seal, with unintelligible inscription. From house 89.

6. Hemispherical limestone spindle whorl, with mark.

H

7. Dog (?) of partly baked dark clay; from archaic stratum in the Temple (?)

8. Dark partly-baked clay object, perhaps a doll; from the charcoal-discoloured stratum outside the east angle of the Temple.

9. Hemispherical limestone spindle whorl inscribed with mark.

10. Dog of unbaked, or partly-baked clay, from the charcoal-discoloured stratum, eastern quarter of the Temple.

11. Hemispherical limestone spindle whorl, with mark, or the hieroglyphic *mes*. From one of the houses in the town.

12. Bow of a boat in baked clay, from S.E. quarter of the Temple. Archaic period.

13. Green glazed plaque with the head of a hawk in relief. From house No. 144. IInd or IIIrd Dynasty. Oxford.

14. Terra-cotta vase from Temple, near to where the main deposit was found.

15. Green glazed vase from house No. 144.

16. Rough red baked earthenware object from the archaic strata at the N. angle of the temple enclosure. These objects are met with in graves of the pre-historic period, several were found in the prehistoric cemetery near the fort, and also in the prehistoric cemetery at Ballas. (See *Naqada and Ballas*.) •

PL. LXIV. All from prehistoric cemetery. 1. Pre-historic bowl, outside red polished, the surface stippled with very shallow dents. Inside black. Ethnol. Mus. Camb.

2 and 4. Prehistoric copper borers of square section. Ethnol. Mus. Camb.

3. Two ivory bangles.

5. Calcite hippopotamus. Roughly made out of a flat piece of alabaster or calcite. Hole for suspension. Grave 153. Ethnol. Mus. Camb.

6. Limestone vase with holes for suspension, con-taining many shells of a land mollusc. From painted tomb.

7. Ivory fan handle (?). This appears to be the splay of a feather or grass fan. The stem of the handle was perhaps of wood, but was not found.

8 and 11. Spheroidal limestone spindle whorls.

9. Forked lance of flint. Painted tomb. (See plan, PL. LXVII, at 7.) Oxford.

10. Mace-head of pink limestone. Decoration on one side only. Point broken, showing conchoidal fracture. The surface has been ground and half polished. The hole to receive the handle is coned from 17 m.m. to 10 m.m., the upper opening being

rounded off, as may be seen in the plate. Grave 525. Ethnol. Mus. Camb.

12. Slate palette with traces of green malachite paint. Grave 525. Ethnol. Mus. Camb.

13. Carnelian pebble for use as muller with slate palette. Grave 525. Ethnol. Mus. Camb.

14. Muller of carnelian or jasper pebble.

15. Slate palette, conventionalised bird's head. Traces of green paint on surface.

16. Vase of very hard and heavy material (diorite?). Ethnol. Mus. Camb.

17. Slate palette in the shape of conventionalised double bird's head. Traces of green paint.

19. Slate palette in the shape of a fish.

20. Double vase, of emery rock, which easily scratches quartz.

PL. LXV. Drawing by Mr. Somers Clarke of the S.E. face of the circular revetment. To the right, behind the granite block of Kha-sekhemui, is seen the end of a stone water-channel, and the lower part of a crude brick pavement.

On the lower part of the plate are sketches of the two limestone pillars, situated near the parallel row of stones on the S.W. side of the temple.

The Roman drain is one of several that descended from the floor-level of houses, now destroyed, which used to occupy the south-western part of the temple enclosure.

PL. LXVI. The upper part of the plate shows pottery from the prehistoric cemetery. The large dish is of coarse yellowish-red pottery; the zigzag decoration round the edge is roughly executed. The base is rounded, as may be seen from the drawing. Below it is a fish of yellowish pink ware decorated in dark red. It was found in the grave of a child with a few rough pots, and a small gold spoon; the bowl of the spoon was nearly circular, the handle was a thin rod of gold, soldered on to it with gold solder.

The wavy handle jar decorated in red has been here reproduced, as it may be a new type.

Below the prehistoric pottery, on the left, is a small doll of baked clay, which was found slightly below the level of the foot of the temple walls in the S.W. quarter; as this doll seems to belong to the period between the Middle and New Kingdoms, it is valuable as evidence for dating the crude brick temple.

To the right of the doll are shown details of the carved serpentine macehead found by Mr. Quibell, and figured in vol. i. on PL. XIX. 6. It has been fitted to the end of a rod, also of serpentine; from the top of this rod a copper pin projects upwards, and may have entered a hole on the upper part now broken off. The horizontal copper pin was introduced from the outside through a small hole afterwards closed by a serpentine stopper. The carving has been carried over the plug or stopper, thus effectually concealing it.

At the bottom of the plate are various types of pots. From the foundation deposit at the N. angle of the temple; they were all wheel-made, and quite new; the shading shows the manner in which they had been scraped to finish the lower part.

[These date from the VIth Dynasty (see *Denderah*, XVI. 24, 27), and point to a rebuilding by Pepy, whose statue was found here.—F. P.]

PL. LXVII. Plan and section of the painted tomb, figured in PLS. LXXV.-LXXVIII. Pot-marks from prehistoric pottery. Pottery models of flint knife and forked lance, the blades painted with red ochre, the handles with black, on which are traces of string or matting, perhaps originally around the handle. Found in a prehistoric grave by Mr. Quibell.

Front and side elevation, and plan, of granite stele at the S.E. side of the temple.

Details of sandstone cornice and polygonal column, from close to the N.W. face of the sanctuary walls.

PL. LXVIII. The sketch shows the vase-grinder's workshop, with the borers resting in the sockets on the earth bench. Below is a plan of the houses examined, drawn to a scale of 1 : 300.

In group 89, in room 5, the dotted line along the wall represents a horizontal hole or drain, the purpose of which was not ascertained. The thin lines in some of the rooms show where the floors are at different levels, or where partition walls were of less height than the actual walls.

In the lowest part of the plate is a sketch of a tomb, which has already been described as occurring at the N. end of the prehistoric cemetery, near the cultivation. The brickwork which surrounds the inner stone chamber is built of small bricks (see Table, p. 23). The stones of which the chamber is built are natural slabs of Nubian sandstone roughly squared. The tomb had been plundered, and nothing but a few fragments of alabaster bowls were found within it.

PL. LXIX. 1–11. All the pottery in the upper part of the plate is from the prehistoric cemetery, and all are variations of types already known. The letters and numbers refer to the scheme of types of pre-historic pottery given in *Naqada and Ballas*. The

large jar with the handle is of rough yellowish red ware. It had been broken, and repaired by drilling holes and tying the parts together.

12–14 come from the "outlier." They belong to about the IIIrd Dynasty.

15. A rough earthenware pot, examples of which were found both in the outlier as well as in the houses.

16. A coarse pottery jar-stand, many of which were found in the houses, as well as in what appears to have been a kiln on the outlier.

17, 18, 19. Three coarse earthenware pots with pointed bases; these were of common occurrence in houses.

20, 21, 23. The two bowls and the dish with the small base were found together in house 211. The bowls are of fine red ware.

22. The pot stand came from one of the houses in the northern angle of the town.

All this pottery from the town belongs to the same period as the seals, that is from the end of the IInd to the beginning of the IVth Dynasty.

[Some, probably, of the Ist Dynasty.—F. P.]

PL. LXX. Inscriptions from clay sealings found in the houses or in the archaic stratum under the temple.

PL. LXXI. Inscriptions from clay sealings found in the houses or in the archaic stratum.

At the bottom of the plate are inscriptions from archaic cylinders, and from an inscribed spindle whorl (PL. LXIII. 1). The wooden cylinder was found by Mr. Quibell during the first season's work.

PL. LXXII. The plan of the temple was executed as follows: Three surveying poles were set up on a straight line parallel to the S.E. wall of the enclosure, the distances being measured by means of a 25 m. steel tape. The surveying poles were 40 m. apart. The total distance between the extreme ends of this base was then 80 m., which is almost exactly that of the inner enclosure wall at this point. Perpendiculars were then laid out from each of these rods by means of a cross-staff. These perpendiculars were marked on the ground by pegs 20 m. apart. It was thus a very easy matter to find the co-ordinate of any point, by means of the cross-staff and two steel tapes 25 m. long. The following description of the discoveries on this site is by Mr. Quibell.

The northern part of the enclosure is seen to be nearly blank. The original surface was lower here than elsewhere, and the bed of earth above the basal sand was very thin. It contained a few large water-

H 2

jars (? XVIIIth Dynasty) standing upright, and at some distance one from the other; no traces of walls were near them; probably they were the water-jars of huts erected in the temple area. Some fragments of glaze kohl tubes with coloured inlay, exactly similar to those dated to Amenhotep II., a slate stele showing Isis and the local god (PL. XLVI. 11), and lastly, a Roman lamp, complete the list of objects found in the upper layer of earth in this part. Below was the sand containing nothing but chips of flint and sherds of the early red and black pottery. Here then the early monuments have evidently been cleared away.

Most of the walls on the plan are of brick and of uniform character.

Two sandstone columns on the W., a short length of wall, also of sandstone, in the centre, and a few scattered blocks of granite, form the only remains of the stone temple.

The revetment and some detached bits of wall at a low level are indeed made of stone, but of thin slabs with unworked surfaces and put together without mortar; but these are on a lower level than the brick walls and may have nothing to do with the temple.

Of the brick walls the one running N. and S. on the W. of the plan is the wall of the town; that on the E. separates the temple from the town itself. The walls do not really run N. and S., but more nearly N.W. and S.E. Our workmen always spoke of them as N. and S., and for convenience the right side of the map will be taken as N. and the top as W.

In the centre is a row of five brick chambers: below the middle one (see top of PL. XLII.) stood the golden-headed hawk; below the next but one to the E. was the second group, that of the copper statues, etc.; and the third and greatest group, marked "Main Deposit," occurred under the group of chambers to the S.E. of the last.

The most striking feature on the plan is the revetment: this was traced on three sides, but on the N. it does not now exist. Two sketches of it are published: one (PL. IV.) from above the U-shaped wall to the S. of the revetment, the other (PL. LXV.) is from the middle of the front, where a wider clearance had been made.

Over the top of the revetment ran a stone trough, consisting of three pieces joined end to end (marked "water channel"). Another piece of the same kind was built into the base of the boundary wall at a point near the S.W. corner; and a third fragment occurred on the sand at the lowest level of the main

deposit in the chamber next to the Pepy stele. This last was in contact with a ring of stone, apparently the coping-stone of a well. It lay on the sand 1·20 m. below the base of the brick walls.

This well was not further examined, as it would have been necessary to destroy the walls for some metres round in order to descend further with safety.

Near the westernmost of the five chambers one of the inscribed maces was found (PL. XXVIA). It was only 1 m. below the surface and lay in a mass of limestone chips, at a higher level than most of the archaic objects. The chips of the poor limestone with conchoidal fracture, which lay in considerable quantities in this part, and round the granite blocks of Khasekhemui, but not elsewhere, show that a very early temple of limestone existed here. These granite blocks of Khasekhemui lay just to the S. of the revetment and at a high level.

The revetment then was already buried when Khasekhemui's temple was built; unless indeed the blocks were dragged up from below, at some time of reconstruction. [Or unless the revetment was from the first intended to consolidate the foundation of Khasekhemui's temple.—F. P.]

A little to the S.E. of the main deposit, and probably forming a part of it, were the two limestone statues, of which one is figured in PL. II. The other was a mere ruin, but enough remained to show that it was the counterpart of the one photographed.

The pair were 2 m. apart, both facing E.; they had probably stood at the entrance of some building, the more so as the human-headed door socket was not far behind them, and close to it was part of a low-level wall made of those small bricks which both here and at El Kab are characteristic of the Old Kingdom.

Just behind these statues and at the level of their base was a group of small objects—a limestone ape, a piece of green glaze, and a coarse vase containing two kinds of beads, glazed spirals (PL. XXIV.), and a single rough, disc-shaped bead of obsidian, about 2 c.m. in diameter.

This serves to date these roughly-chipped obsidian discs to the early period. Many of them were found in the temple at various points, but always at low levels. I have not seen them elsewhere in Egypt.

Two of the large stone vases were at some distance from the main deposit.

The great alabaster vase of Khasekhem stood midway down the E. side, and at the top of it, at a higher level, therefore, than most of the archaic objects ; and the uninscribed spherical vase of syenite (PL. XXXVII.) was at the S.E. corner of the revetment, a little N. of the main deposit.

A little to the N. of this were two rude stone pillars, about 1 m. high, pointed at the top, like rough obelisks.

Just to the S. of this vase lay the great stele of Pepy. This is a tall granite pillar, 3·25 m. (10 ft. 8 ins.) in height, rectangular in section, rounded at the top. The lower, ·65 m., is left in the rough and must have served to fix the pillar in the ground. The upper, 1·25 m., is inscribed on one side with the figure and name of a Pepy, but the cutting is very shallow and the inscription much defaced. This object has not yet been removed. It was found lying much on the same level as the great deposit, and to the S. of it.

Leaving now this part of the plan, we see on the W. a group of columns, or, rather, of the brickwork pits in which the bases of the columns once stood ; stone blocks remained in two of them only.

Near them was found a granite altar of Amenhotep IV., but this had probably been moved in modern times ; the *fellahin* knew of its existence.

At a point to the N.W. of these columns was a scattered foundation deposit ; it consisted of four rude vases (PL. XLIX. 18), green glaze beads, both cylindrical and disc-shaped, and a rectangular plaque of green glaze, with the name of Thothmes III. written in black ink. This is important as giving a date to the brick walls near it, and therefore possibly to the period at which the archaic objects were buried.

In the middle of the plan towards the S. two large masses of brickwork are marked. They must have been the cores of a pylon ; two of the facing blocks were found adhering. This pylon would be fairly in line with the granite sill of the door on the E. side ; but the northern part of the temple seems to have faced S.

Small circular buildings, often with very thin walls, occurred at various points ; they are marked on the map, but are probably only granaries, and not connected with the temple. Some, however, were at a low level ; none are modern.

The untouched soil beneath the temple is a bed of very clean sand, generally reached at about 2 m. from the surface ; but in some parts, holes of over 4 m. in depth had to be dug.

In the upper part of this bed of sand, fine flint flakes, charcoal, and fragments of the Naqada types of pottery were scattered.

Lower down the signs of human action were rarer, but I never got really below them even at 3 m. depth in the sand.

Above the sand came a layer of black clay, containing again archaic pottery. Over this, in the S.W. quarter of the temple, was an artificial layer of sand, 55 c.m. thick. On this came the brick walls, and the surface layer contained great quantities of sandstone fragments from the temple, with limestone chip only in the part near the Kha-sekhemui blocks.

Here may be added the names of later kings of whom monuments were found.

Of Pepy II. there was part of the base of a small statue in yellow limestone. A reworked lintel, found high above the main deposit of archaic objects, and another sandstone block bearing a cartouche, came from Usertesen I.

Of Thothmes III., besides the foundation deposit and the blocks of the pylon, we found the trunk of a statue in basalt. Next comes the granite altar of Amenhotep IV., a fragment from the base of a statue of Sety I., the cartouche of Rameses II., and a block with the three names of Rameses X., which completes the list.

There was curiously little that could be dated to a late period, but in the N.W. of the temple was a Roman pavement, and several pieces of Roman pottery were found along the W. side. Nothing then was done for the temple after the late New Kingdom. Mr. Green further describes the site.

The district of El Kab and Kom el Ahmar is near to the junction between the limestone and the underlying Nubian sandstone.

The actual junction being about 5 kilometres N. of El Kab on the E. bank, but owing to the bend of the Nile and the slightly westerly trend of the limestone cliff near Esna, a large expanse of Nubian sandstone is exposed on the W. bank. There is a dip from N.E. to S.W. of this rock ; so that, while on the E. bank it forms hills from 80 to 90 metres, and, in places, 156 m. high, on the W. bank it does not exceed 30 m. above the cultivation.

The top of these hills, as may be seen on the map, is a plateau nearly flat, but intersected by watercourses at its eastern border. The surface, which slopes slightly to the northward, is covered with fine shingle and flint pebbles, weathered to a deep brown-black. That part of the plateau which is nearest to the site has been denuded into a series of detached knolls, some of which have a cap of a hard fossiliferous limestone weathered to a light bluish-grey colour.

Pieces of fossil wood seem to be associated in some way with this limestone, as the fragments that were found were near hills so capped; but no fossil wood was observed *in situ*.

From the cliffs which form the eastern border of the plateau there extends to the cultivation a gentle slope of fine gravel and sand, on which are angular blocks of sandstone. At the S. of the map is a large drainage line, marked out by a line of scrub. No tombs were found S. of this, till the neighbourhood of Edfu was reached.

The cultivation has encroached upon the desert considerably since the prehistoric period, as is shown by sections exposed in wells.

The little knoll seen to the S.E. of the town is an "outlier," having been surrounded by the encroachment of the cultivation. In it were found several jars of the prehistoric or early historic period; and, at the head of the old desert, a prehistoric burial of a child, with a slate palette, several rough pots, and an ostrich egg. The upper part of the knoll is composed of rubbish thrown from a pottery kiln. Much pottery of the early dynasties, such as rough vases with pointed bases, and rough pot stands, were found here, as well as a great number of fragments, partly fused and distorted by heat.

On the N.W. side of the town is another outlier, in which many fragments of prehistoric pottery and flint flakes were found.

These outliers give an idea how extensive was the inhabited district during the prehistoric period.

The map of the district shown on PL. LXXIIIA. is drawn to a scale of 66 m.m. = 1 kilometre, the scale being $\frac{1}{15000}$. The field map from which it was reduced was drawn to a scale of 100 m.m. = 1 kilometre, or R.F. $\frac{1}{10000}$.

A base line 1535 metres long was measured once by means of a steel tape 25 metres long; this measurement agreed well with a previous measurement made by pacing, so that any large error is improbable. The two ends of this base were situated on two small knolls, one at the foot of the hill in which are the rock-cut tombs of the New Kingdom, and the other at the foot of the low cliffs further to the S.E. The principal points were then fixed by a triangulation executed by means of a box sextant reading to 1' of arc.

The positions of points thus fixed agree well with observations made from points on the El Kab side of the river, which in turn had been fixed by means of a triangulation made in 1896.

The details were filled in by means of a small improvised plane-table, prismatic compass bearings, and sketches executed to a much larger scale on a cavalry sketching-board.

The absolute heights having no direct bearing on the work, it was not judged needful to expend the time necessary to representing the hill features by means of contours; they are therefore shown by form lines only, but any question regarding the visibility or invisibility of one point from another, can, owing to the simple character of the district, be answered with sufficient accuracy by inspection of the form lines.

The true N. was not established with accuracy, but this will not be of much consequence, as soon as the survey of the Nile Valley, now being executed by the Government, comes to be published.

The magnetic variation for the year 1899 was more probably $3\frac{1}{2}°$ W. than $4°$ W. as shown.

PL. LXXIV. For the description of the fort see chapter vi., by Mr. Somers Clarke.

PLS. LXXV.–LXXVIII. These paintings of the prehistoric tomb are fully described in sections 52, 53, and 54.

[The age of this tomb is given in sequence dates by the pottery, as follows :—

Type D. 8, sequence date	31–61
„ W. 41 „ „	63, 64
„ R. 81 „ „	38–80
„ P. 40 „ „	34–70
„ R. 94 „ „	49–53
„ R. 24 „ „	42–80
„ R. 1E „ „	51–63
„ B. 42 „ „	31–70

Here R. 94 is the only type which clashes, as not being yet known beyond S. D. 53; but it might well go rather later. And thus we can date this tomb best by the well-defined type of W. 41, which belongs to S. D. 63.—F. P.]

CHAPTER XIV.

THE CLAY SEALINGS.

BY F. LL. GRIFFITH, F.S.A.

THE seals on PL. LXX.–LXXI, discovered by Mr. Quibell and Mr. Green at Hierakonpolis, form an interesting and important addition to the scanty epigraphic material for the earliest dynasties. As yet these inscriptions are very difficult to interpret; and it is always possible that, as was certainly the case in later times, the engraver of seals used hieroglyphs merely to form designs or patterns that were verbally quite meaningless, but none the less were distinctive to their possessor. A certain number of important groups or signs already known can be recognised with ease; and no doubt when taken in connection with the whole find at Hierakonpolis, and with similar discoveries elsewhere, more can be said of the collection than can be given in the following brief notes, written on these two plates alone, and far from books of reference. Prof. Petrie informs me that none of the seals are identical with any from Abydos, and that most seem to him to date from the IInd or IIIrd Dynasty.

Fig. 1. The Horus name, Kha-ba, of an early king, already known from a sealing in Prof. Petrie's collection, published in his 'History of Egypt.'

Fig. 2. Neb-maat, the Horus name of King Senefru, IVth Dynasty.

Fig. 3. Neter-Khet or Khet-Neter, of King Zeser of the IIIrd Dynasty. The accompanying signs *Khet-Khen* are of very uncertain meaning.

Fig. 8. Here we see the hawk of the god of Hierakonpolis, in the XIIth nome of Upper Egypt, nearly opposite Asyût. This bird deity appears also as an element in the name-cartouche of Merenra of the VIth dynasty.

Fig. 10. A proper name, Chnem (?)-hotep, which recurs in fig. 11, is preceded by a title *mater* found as late as the IVth Dynasty, but probably most common in the IIIrd Dynasty.

Figs. 14–16. In these the word *hbn* "ebony" occurs, probably as a proper name. In 14 there is also the title *mater*.

Fig. 18, 19. The sign for scribe is followed by its usual reading *sesh* (for *sekh*?) in alphabetic characters.

Fig. 22. Probably to be read the *mater* Sesa.

Fig. 24. This may contain a group *hotep neterui*; compare the titles of Khasekhemui in *Royal Tombs*, Pt. II.

Figs. 26–32. These legends contain the symbol of the goddess Neith, already found at Abydos in inscriptions of the Ist Dynasty.

Fig. 39. This fragment may perhaps include the title *semer-uati*, "confidential friend of the king."

INDEX.

	PAGE
Alabaster votive dishes, small, PLS.	
XXX., XXXIV. . . 14, 32, 43	
Amenhotep IV., altar of . . . 53	
Antef 11	
Anu, festival of destruction of 24, 42	
Barsanti, M. 28, 46	
Beads, unfinished 12	
„ discs of obsidian, PL.	
XXIV. 52	
Besh 24	
Bissing, Freiherr von . . . 35	
Borchardt, Dr. . . 28, 44, 46	
Borers for stone vases, PLS.	
XXXII., LXII. . . . 49	
Bricks, crude, table of dimensions	
of 23	
Bucrania 37	
Capart, M. 42	
Charcoal-discoloured stratum	
2, 3, 9-12	
Clarke, Mr. Somers 24	
Colours used in prehistoric paint-	
ing 21	
Copper chisel and adze . . . 26	
Cylinder seal, baked clay, PL.	
LXIII. 49	
Cylinder seal, wooden, PL. LXXI.	
26, 51	
Dahshur, treasure 45	
Deposit, main 2	
„ „ catalogue of 30, 33, 52	
Desert surface 2	
„ „ reached by excava-	
tions 1	
„ „ underlying site . 4	
Doll, clay (XII.–XVIII. Dynasty),	
PL. LXVL 18, 50	

	PAGE
Door-socket, human-headed, PL.	
III. 34, 36	
Drains, Roman, PL. LXV. . 9, 50	
Dwarf, grave of 26	
„ ivory figure of, PL. XI. . 37	
Elephants on carved ivory . . 34	
Erman, Professor 43	
Face-paint, malachite 42	
Flint implements, minute . . . 11	
Flint, great, PL. III. 1, 2 . . 36	
Flint knives, models of . . . 26	
Floors, crude brick 9	
Flower, Capt. 41	
Fort, PL. LXXIV. 54	
„ date of 25	
Fossil wood 54	
Foundation deposit of Thothmes	
III. 33, 53	
Granaries 11	
„ Old Kingdom . . . 25	
Graves, "Pan" of Hu . . . 22	
„ prehistoric, in town area . 2	
„ „ cemetery . . 22	
„ „ with compart-	
ments for offerings . . 22, 26	
Greek island figures 38	
Green, Mr. F. W. . . . 24, 40	
Griffith, Mr. F. Ll. 54	
Handle of alabaster jar, archaic,	
PL. LIX., 3 . . . . 9, 48	
Hawk, golden-headed, PLS. XLII.,	
XLIII., XLVII. . . 27, 33, 44	
Haworth, Mr. Jesse 24	
Heuzey, M. 43	
Hierakonpolis district, PL. LXXIIIA.	
53, 54	

	PAGE
Hippopotamus, calcite, PL. LXIV. 50	
Houses, in town area 2	
„ remains of under wall . 2	
Houses, Old Kingdom . . . 16	
Hügel, Baron von 49	
Human sacrifice (Tikanou) . . 40	
Iron, wrought 11	
Ivory, carved, PLS. V.–XVI. 29, 36, 38	
Ivory, deposit of 29	
Kha-ba 3	
„ „ sealing of, PL. LXX. . . 55	
Kha-sekhem, statue and stele of . 2	
„ „ statue of, PLS. XL.,	
XLI. . . . 28, 33, 34, 44	
„ „ stele of, PL. LVIII.	
10, 47	
„ „ granite vase of, PLS.	
XXXVI., XXXVIII. 29, 31, 43,	
44	
„ „ alabaster, PLS.	
XXXVII., XXXVIII. . 43, 44	
„ „ alabaster bowl of 11, 31	
Kha-sekhemui, fragment of vase	
of, PL. LIX. 8 . . . 10, 48	
„ „ door jamb of,	
PLS. IL., XXIII., LXV. 35, 39, 50	
Khebs-ta, ceremony 41	
Khet-Neter or Neter-Khet (Zeser),	
monument of, at Berlin . 25, 38	
Khufu, bowl of, PL. XVIII., 6 . 38	
Kom el Ahmar 24, 25	
Lance-head, forked pattern, PL.	
LXIV. 21, 50	
Limestone block, circular . . 2, 6	
Lion, pottery, PLS. XLIV., XLV.	
27, 28, 45	

PAGE

Mace, Mr. A. C. 24
Mace-heads, decorated, PLS. XXVI.
   A, B, C 39-41
   ,, ,, double ram's head,
     PL. XXV. . . . . . ,38
   ,, ,, ivory, PL. XXII. 4 . 37
   ,, ,, carved serpentine,
     PLS. XXIII., LXVI. . 39, 50
Magnetic variation 54
Main deposit 13, 29, 33
Map of district, PL. LXXIII A. 53, 54
Maspero, Professor . . . 40, 41
Mastabas, Old Kingdom . . . 25
   ,,   ,, bricks of 23
Mena tomb, flints from . . 39, 43
Morgan, M. de 45
Murray, Miss 24

Nails, gold 35, 45
Nar-mer 24
   ,, ,, inscribed ivory of, PL.
     XV. 7 . . . . . 34, 37
   ,, ,, palette of, PL. XXIX. 13, 41
   ,, ,, reading of name of . 42
Naville, Dr. 36, 42
Neb-Maat (Snefru) 55
Necho 11
Nekhen, hieroglyphic sign of . 3
Neter-Khet or Khet-Neter (Zeser) 3
New Kingdom, tombs of . . . 25
Numerals 41, 43

Old Kingdom, decorated tombs of 25
Orientation of prehistoric graves . 22
Outlier 54

Palermo stone 42
Palette, great, PL. XXIX. . 29, 41
  ,, small, PL. XXVIII. . 41
Palettes, decorated prehistoric . 42
Pan graves. 22, 37
Parallel rows of stones . . . 7
Pavements, low level . . . 2
   ,, rough stone . . . 7
   ,, crude brick . . . 9
Peers, Mr. 24
Pepy 28
  ,, statue of 33
Pepy I. 34, 45
Pepy II. 53
Pepy, granite stele of 53

Pepy, copper statue of . . . 27
  ,, description of copper statue
    of, PLS. L.-LVI. . . . 46
Petrie, Professor 8, 24
Pillars 2, 8
Pirie, Miss A. A. 24
Plaque, green glaze, decorated . 18
   ,,   ,,   ,, PL.
     LXIII. 50
   ,,   ,,   ,, Old Kingdom,
     PL. XVIII., 2 . . 25, 38
Pottery, New Kingdom . . . 10
   ,, long vessels with ashes . 10
   ,, incised, XII.-XVIII.
     Dynasty 16
   ,, Roman or Coptic . . 9
Prehistoric tomb-painting, PLS.
   LXXV.-LXXIX. . . 20, 21
Pylons 2, 33

Quartz, green glazed, PL. XXIV. 39
Quibell, Mr. J. E. 2, 11

Revetment, circular 2, 3
   ,, date of 5
   ,, depth of . 7, 33, 52
Revetted blind passage . . . 6
Revetted inclined plane . . 2, 5
Roman drains, PL. LXV. . 9, 50
   ,, pavement 53
   ,, pottery 53
Rubbish shoot 11

Sanctuary chambers 52
Schweinfurth, Dr. 35
Sealings 16
   ,, description of, PLS. LXX.,
     LXXI. 54
Sebek-hotep 11
Sections 4, 12
Sed festival, PL. LXIV. . 34, 45
Sety I. 53
Shunet ez Zebib . . . 20, 25
Slab, rectangular 29
Snefru 3
Spindle whorls 17
   ,,   ,, spheroidal, PL.
     XLIV. 22, 50
Stairway tomb 25
Standards with symbols of deities 42

Statue, large copper, PL. XLVII.
                   27, 45
   ,, small copper, PLS. L.-LVI.
                   28, 46
   ,, head of small limestone,
     PL. V. 36
   ,, archaic, PL. LVII. . 15, 47
Statues, limestone, PLS. I., II. 33-35
Statuette, archaic, PL. LIX. 1, 11, 48
Stele, rough uninscribed granite . 10
  ,, of Pepy 53
  ,, Kha-sekhem 10
Store rooms 10
Strata 1, 2, 3
Structures, archaic . . . 7, 19

Temple, archaic 7, 36
   ,, crude brick (XVIIIth
     Dynasty ?) 2
   ,,   ,,   ,, general depth
     of walls of . . . 3-6
   ,,   ,,   ,, plan of, PL.
     LXXII. 51
Thothmes III., sandstone architrave of 11
   ,,   ,, foundation de-
     posit of 33
   ,,   ,, scarab of . . 10
Tile, green glaze, PL. XXXII. 2 . 43
Tylor, Mr. J. J. 24

Usertesen I. 15, 53

Vase, alabaster, PL. LIX. 2 . 10, 48
  ,,   ,, of Kha-sekhem . 52
  ,, Great Syenite, PL. XXXVII.
                   33, 43

Walls, early crude brick . . 6
  ,, parallel enclosure . . . 9
  ,, skewed 3
Water-channel 52
Water-level 5
Well 6, 9, 52
Workshop, vase-grinder's, PL.
   LXVIII. 17, 51

Zeser, Khet-Neter 55
Zet, PL. LIX. 48

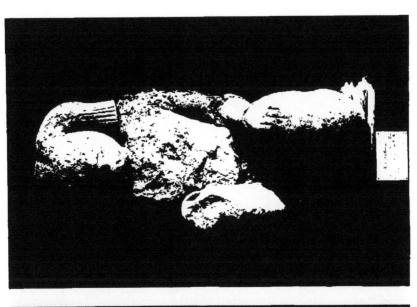

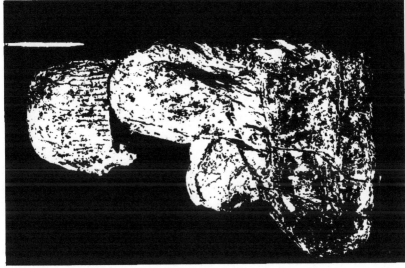

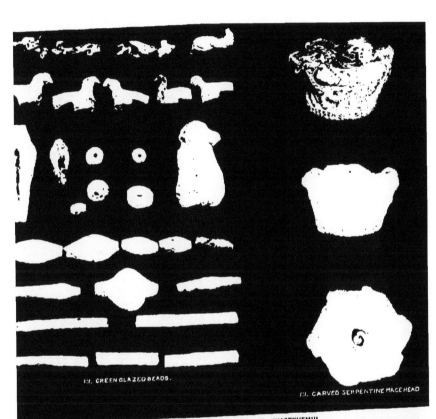

1:1. GREEN GLAZED BEADS.

1:1. CARVED SERPENTINE MACE HEAD

1:4 INSCRIPTION FROM BLOCK OF KHASEKHEMUI.

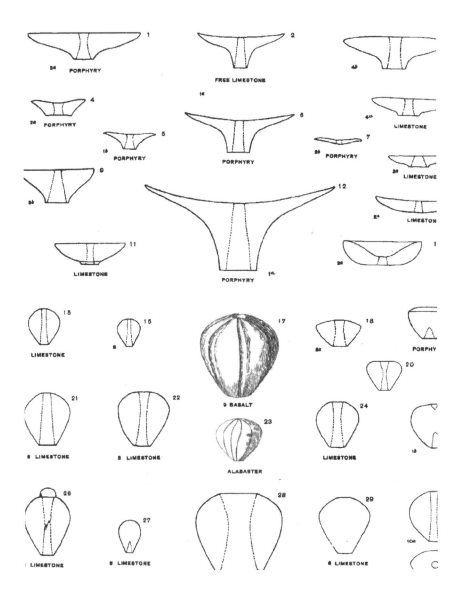

1   PORPHYRY

2   FREE LIMESTONE

4   PORPHYRY

5   PORPHYRY

6   PORPHYRY

7   PORPHYRY

LIMESTONE

LIMESTONE

LIMESTONE

9

12   PORPHYRY

11   LIMESTONE

15   LIMESTONE

16

17   9 BASALT

18

PORPHY

20

21   8 LIMESTONE

22   8 LIMESTONE

23   ALABASTER

24   LIMESTONE

26   I LIMESTONE

27   8 LIMESTONE

28

29   8 LIMESTONE

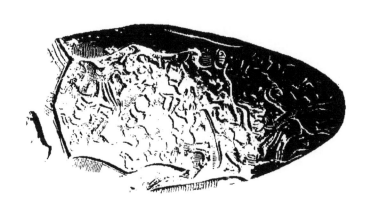

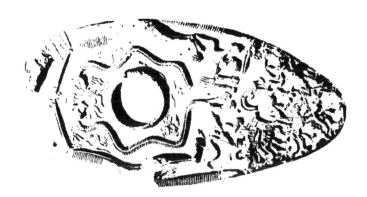

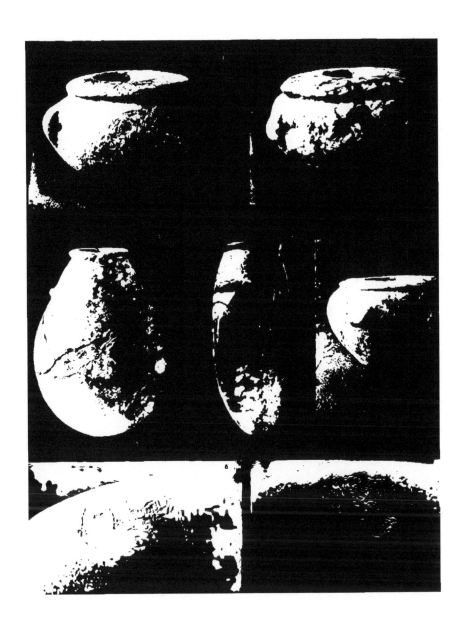

CHERT APE.

UPPER AND UNDER SURFACE OF GREEN GLAZE

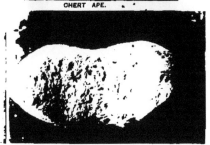

CHERT VASE GRINDER.

HÆMATITE SCORPION.

INSCRIBED IVORY FROM MAIN DEPOSIT.

COPPER STATUE. POTTERY LION AND SCHIST STATUE.

1:4 GOLD HEADED HAWK SHOWING RIVETS.

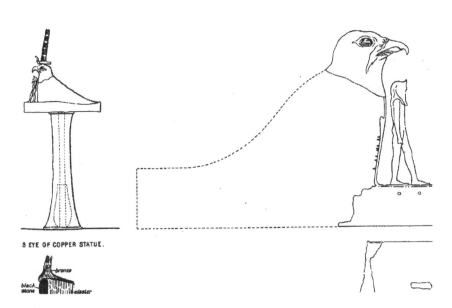

3 EYE OF COPPER STATUE.

bronze

black
stone

alaster

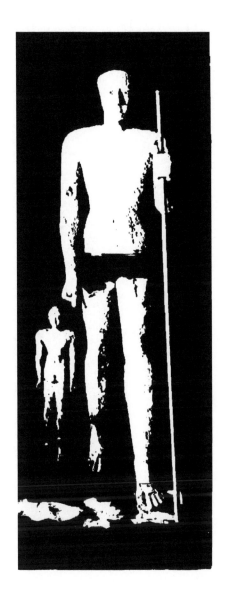

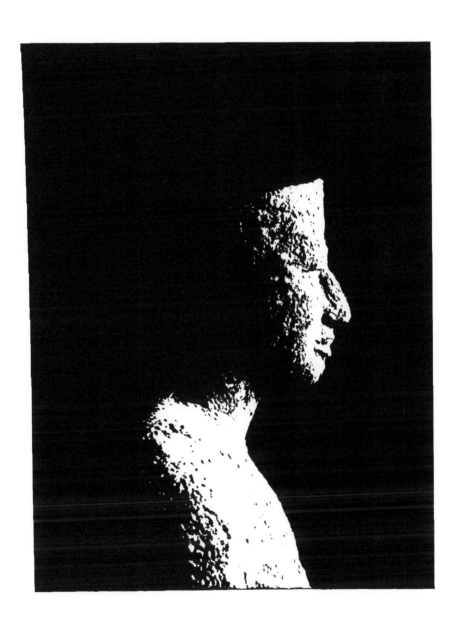

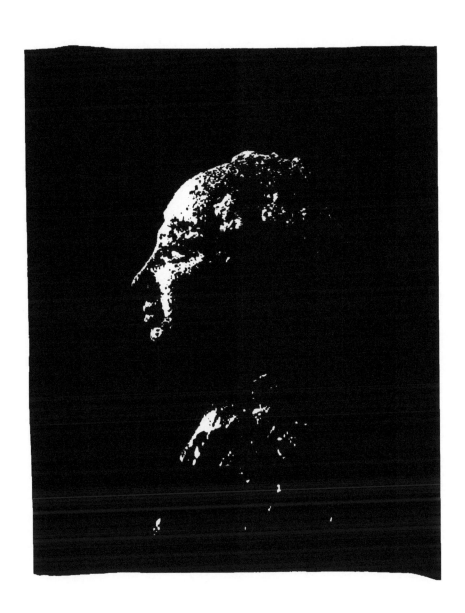

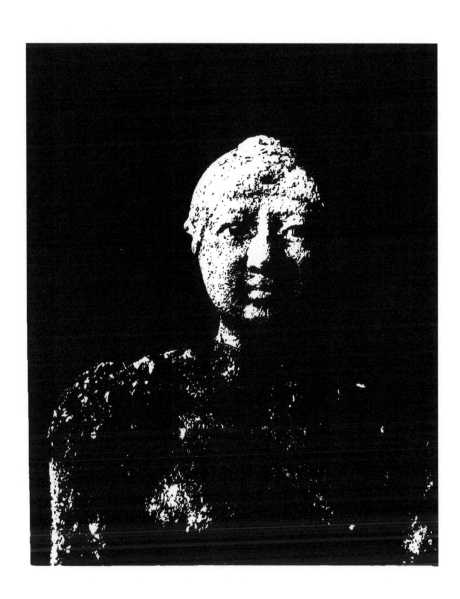

KNIVES FROM TEMPLE SITE.

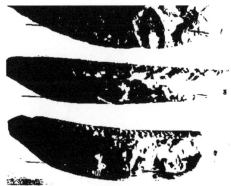

1 : 2

1 : 2

1 : 3

TERRA COTTA HEAD OF APE.

TERRA COTTA HEAD OF DONKEY.

1:2 DIORITE VASE GRINDER, UNDERSIDE.

. 1:3 DIORITE VASE GRINDER, IN POSITIO
ON BLOCK OF QUARTZ CRYSTAL.

2:3 SPINDLE WHORLES AND CLAY MODELS.

1:3 TERRA COTTA BOAT.

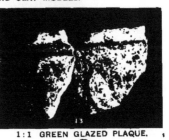

1:1 GREEN GLAZED PLAQUE.

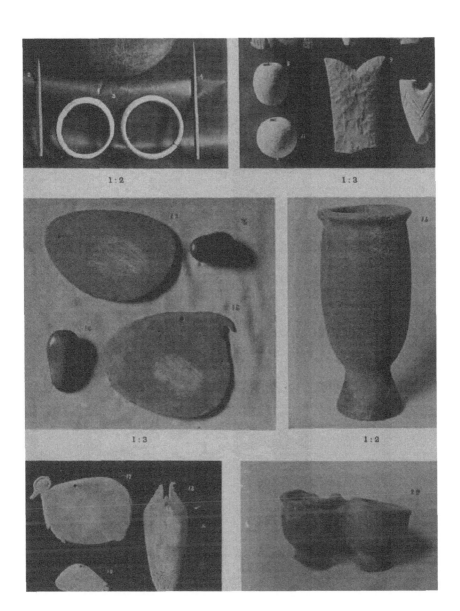

1:2   1:3

1:3   1:2

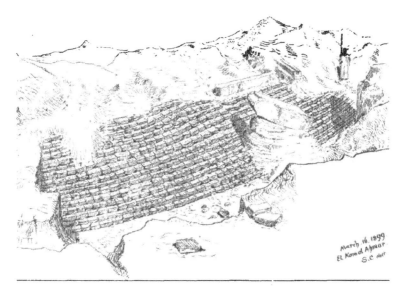

S.E. FACE OF REVETMENT AND INSCRIBED BLOCK OF KHASEKHEMUI.

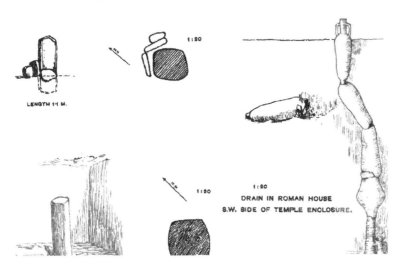

LENGTH 1·1 M.

1:20

1:20

1:20

DRAIN IN ROMAN HOUSE
S.W. SIDE OF TEMPLE ENCLOSURE.

RED LINES

DECORATED IN RED

1:4 PREHISTORIC CEMETERY

:1 TERRA-COTTA DOLL

DETAILS OF CARVED SERPENTINE MACE-HEAD
METAL SHOWN IN BLACK ABOUT 1:1

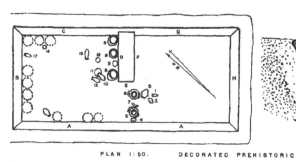

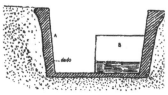

PLAN 1:50.   DECORATED PREHISTORIC TOMB.

TRANSVERSE SECTION 1:50.

1. H. 52. limestone	7. Flint lance	13. R. I.	The jars shown dotted
2. H. 27. diorite	8. R. 81	14. R. I. a.	were probable R. 81.
3. D. 8.	9. P. 40	15. R. 94	
4. Shell	10. R. 94	16.	
5 W. 41	11. R. 24	17. B. 42	
6 W. 41	12. R. 94	18. R. 84	

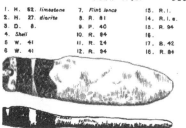

on P 56 a
grave 605.

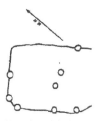

1:50 GRAVE 500. SHOWING SOCKETS

on bottom of P. II. c.
grave 527.   bottom of P. 56. a. grave 167.

1. 2 POTTERY MODELS OF
FLINT KNIFE AND LANCE.

1. 2 PREHISTORIC POT MARKS.

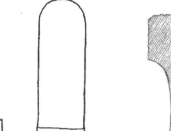

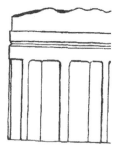

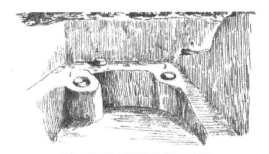

VASE MAKER'S WORKSHOP, WITH BENCH.
1. VASE GRINDER IN EARTHEN SOCKET   2. CORN GRINDER   3. VASE GRINDER
4. STONE DOOR SOCKET.

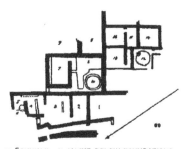

10. "SHUNA"   11. MAJUR BELOW FOUNDATIONS
12. VASE GRINDER'S WORKSHOP

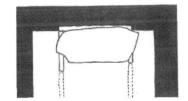

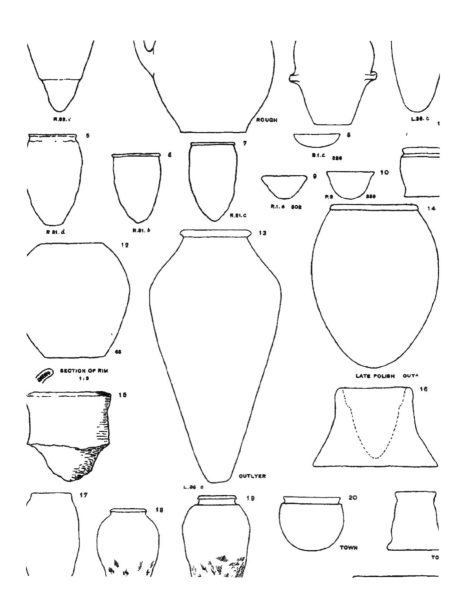

pot seal

an knot of reeds

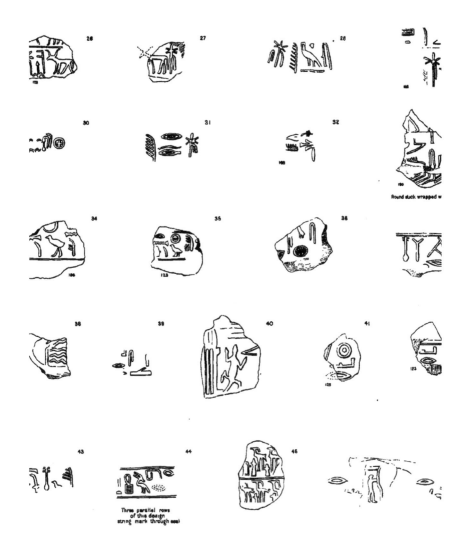

Round stuck wrapped w

Three parallel rows
of this design
string mark through seal

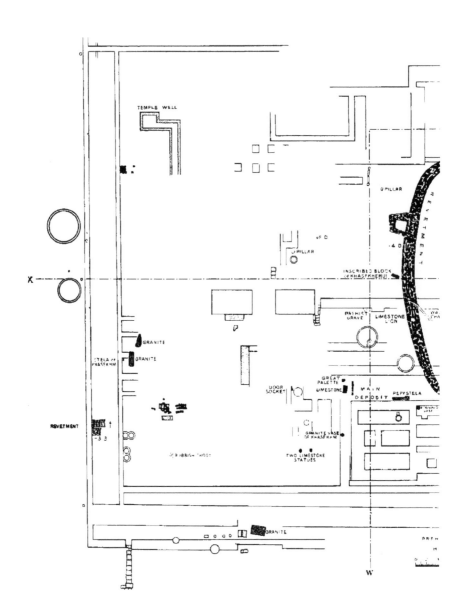

TEMPLE WELL

REVETMENT

O PILLAR

O PILLAR

OF D

INSCRIBED BLOCK
OF KHASEKHEMUI

X

PREHIST
GRAVE

LIMESTONE
LION

GRANITE

GRANITE

STELA OF
KHASEKHM

GREAT
PALETTE

DOOR
SOCKET

LIMESTONE

MAIN
DEPOSIT

PEPY STELA

REVETMENT

GRANITE VASE
OF KHASEKHM

OF RUBBISH SHOOT

TWO LIMESTONE
STATUES

GRANITE

PREH

W

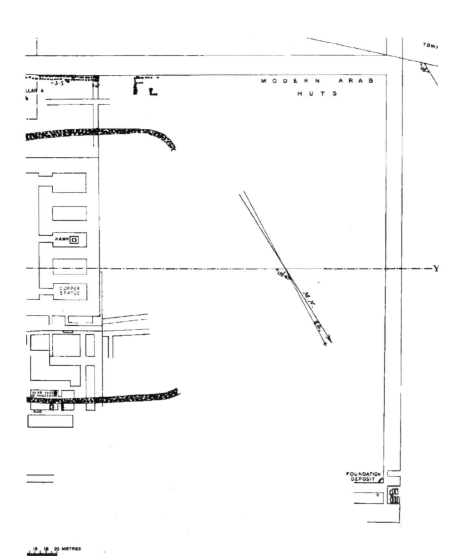

TOWI

−3·5

LLAR A

L

MODERN ARAB
HUTS

HAWK

COPPER
STATUE

M.N.

ARAB VASE
OF KHALEAN

FOUNDATION
DEPOSIT

0

10 15 20 METRES

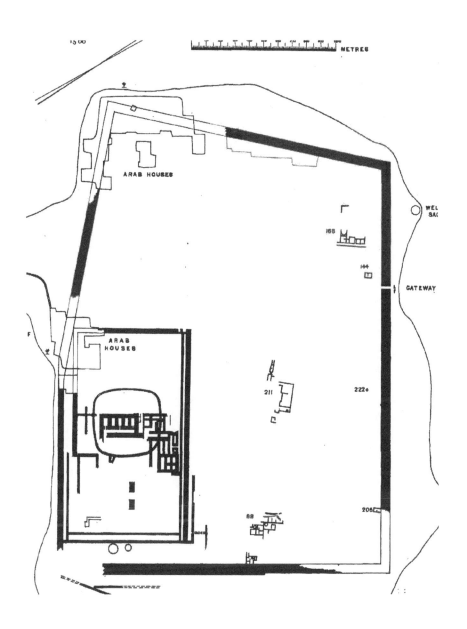

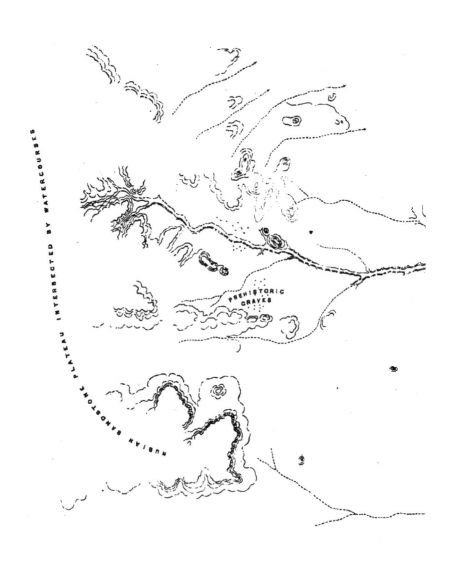

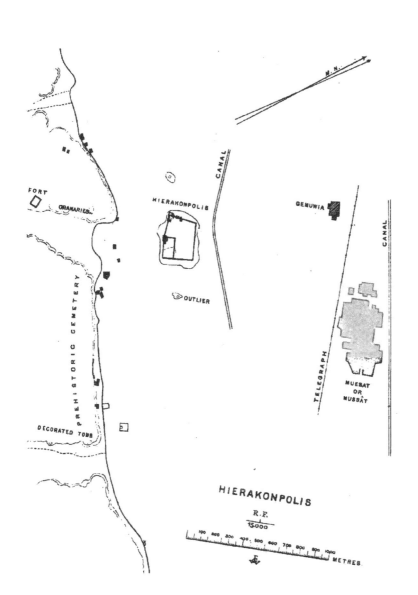

HIERAKONPOLIS

R.F.
$\frac{1}{15\cdot000}$

METRES.

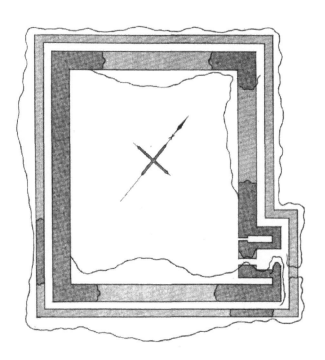

0 10 20 30 40 50 60 70 80 90 100 FEET

0 5 10 20 30 40 METRES

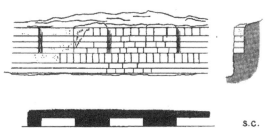

S.C.

A

FWG del

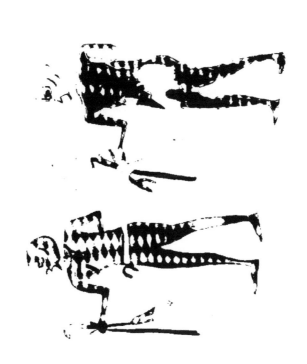

Lightning Source UK Ltd.
Milton Keynes UK
UKHW022331060223
416579UK00001B/127